Majoring In Motherhood

By Barbra Roylance Williams

Majoring in Motherhood

By Barbra Roylance Williams

Copyright © 2012 by Barbra Roylance Williams

Cover Design by: Barbra Roylance Williams

All rights reserved. No part of this publication may be reproduced, stored in or introduced into a retrieval system, transmitted in any form, or used in any manner without the written permission and consent of the author.

This is based on a true story; however, any names or characters used in this book are fictitious.

ISBN-13: 978-1468148985
ISBN-10: 1468148982

Majoring in Motherhood

This book is dedicated to Noah, my darling son, and Samuel, my beloved husband.
I would be so lost without you both.

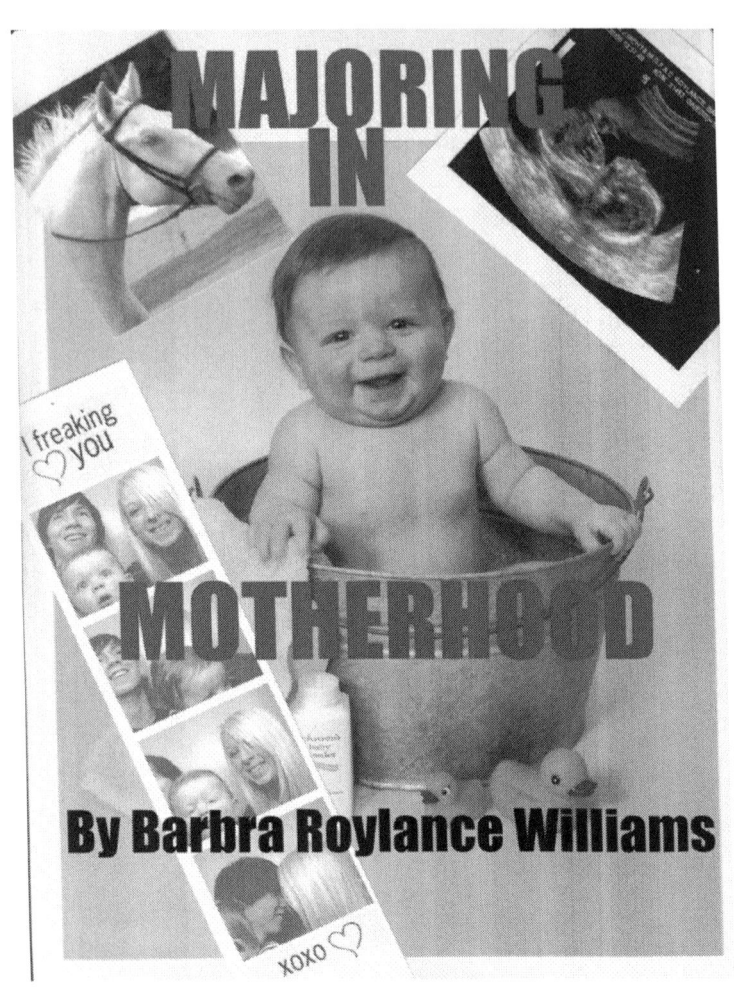

Majoring in Motherhood

Majoring in Motherhood

Prologue

Being a young teenage mother is hard. My eyes are glazing over right now as I sit, and unfold my story to you. You will be forced to make difficult sacrifices that will change your life forever. For some, it will bring a new happiness and love they never knew existed. It will cause hardships and strife that force you to become the strong woman you didn't know you could be. For the weak, it will be just enough to push them over the edge.

You will find that even your closest friends will distance themselves from you and from a baby. You will experience loneliness on a whole new level, but will be able to embrace the sweet innocence that rests between your arms. God is the one who chose to bless you with child, so remember, that baby is meant to be here. Love that baby with all your heart, for he or she is all yours, admires you, and fully depends on you.

Majoring in Motherhood

I dedicate this book to all the young mothers out there who grasped the strength they had inside, and gave up everything to become the best mothers they could be. You must give to receive, and through this book, you will see that I sacrificed everything, but in return, received the greatest gift I've ever been given; my son. You will never experience a love, like the love of your child. With this book, I welcome you into my world. It is the diary of my life.

Chapter One
Elementary School

Have you ever been so lonely that you could feel it physically? I know I have. I was a military brat, having lived in as many houses as I was old. I had been homeschooled, mainly for the reason that we were always moving, but also, because I was quite the handful for a teacher. My parents began schooling me themselves in fifth grade when I got kicked out of a fancy private school for making a teacher go over the deep end.

My teacher, Mrs. Hawkins, had always reserved a deep hate for me and she was not afraid to show it. She consistently called on me during class, just so that she could tell me I was wrong, and gave me extra homework every night. After several months of being mistreated by her, I finally stood up for myself.

As Mrs. Hawkins passed out the one page of homework to my fifth grade class, and then handed me five pages of homework, I threw a fit. How was this fair? None of the other kids had five pages of homework, and I wanted to go home and play! Without one thought to the consequences, I drew all over my homework with a marker as obnoxiously as I could, and then I stood up in front of the entire class. I

Majoring in Motherhood

marched right up to Mrs. Hawkins, ripped my homework to shreds and threw it into the trash can right in front of her. I watched as my teacher's face went from a fair white to a feverish red. I could see the veins pulsing out of her forehead and sweat began to shimmer near her hairline. She glared at me with devilish eyes and I suddenly grew very afraid of her.

As I tried to run back to my desk, she furiously grabbed me by the shoulder and yanked me into the principal's office for the third time that week. I literally used to have a daily visit to the principal's office, mostly because of Mrs. Hawkins, and my little fifth grader reputation was ruined. All the other students thought I was a bad kid.

As Mrs. Hawkins started yelling at the principal to punish me, I grew emotionally upset. Why was I always getting in trouble? Why didn't Mrs. Hawkins like me? What was wrong with me? The principal sneered at me, and then picked up the phone to contact my parents.

"Yes, is this Tim?" asked the principal.

"Yes," replied my dad.

"Your daughter is in my office again. She has had terrible conduct this entire week and I would like to seek your consent in spanking her." The principal peered at me from behind her desk.

"Spank her? For what?" asked my father.

"She has continuously been a class distraction, and she

Majoring in Motherhood

ripped up her homework in front of the entire class today. We can't allow the rest of the students to think that this kind of behavior is acceptable," the principal paused, "Tim, your daughter is a bad influence."

"Do not spank my daughter," my dad replied, "I'll be there in a minute."

My teacher grabbed me by the shoulder, and pulled me out of the principal's office.

"Follow me," she said hastily. I followed her into the gym, where she sat me on the bleachers by myself and made me wait alone. I pondered over what my father would say when he got there.

Thirty long minutes later, the gym doors finally opened, and there stood my dad, the principal, and Mrs. Hawkins. I jumped off the bleachers, and ran to my dad's side. Surely, he would defend me.

"Your daughter is a complete nuisance!" yelled Mrs. Hawkins. My dad turned around to stare my teacher in the face.

"You have no right to yell at me over this," he snapped, "I don't even know the whole story yet." The principal poised herself professionally and approached my father.

"Barbra has been a class distraction almost every day this week, and she's causing the other students to lose their concentration."

"Okay," said my father hesitantly.

Majoring in Motherhood

"Your daughter is a child from hell!" screamed Mrs. Hawkins.

"What!" yelled my dad. He turned around lividly, and locked his eyes on Mrs. Hawkins.

"How dare you say that about my daughter? This is supposed to be a *Christian* school!" shouted Dad. He turned back around to look at me.

"Barbra, get all your things," he said sternly. While I ran back up to the classroom to get all my belongings, my father dis-enrolled me from the private school, and put in a very bad word for my teacher. A couple years later, I heard that Mrs. Hawkins got fired for going crazy again, and ended up in a nut house. I guess you got what you deserved, bitch.

As I grew from child to teenager, I never lost my rebellious streak. I was always against my parents and brothers, and no matter what they said, I always made an effort to do the exact opposite of it. Looking back on my childhood years, I wish that I had been a different kid. I mean, my life hadn't been bad, but it could have been so much better. Maybe those years at home wouldn't have been so difficult, and I possibly could have enjoyed them?

My father, Tim, was a successful pilot for FedEx, who had retired out of the Navy as a Commander. He was a truly respectable man who had graduated from the United States Naval Academy, served twenty years in the Navy as

Majoring in Motherhood

a pilot, and earned many medals as a war veteran. He was an ambitious man, tall with brown hair, nearly a genius in math, and had a seriously short temper for failure.

My mother, Nancy, was a stay at home mom, devoted Christian, and deserved five stars for always keeping our house so clean. She was short, just under five feet tall with curly brown hair and two different colored eyes. She was something to see, but not something to mess with. My mother was known for her dynamite personality, but her small stature fooled almost anyone. What they didn't know was that hiding behind that small body was a warhead that could take you out in one blow. She met my father while he was in the Navy, and it had been true love ever since they'd married nearly twenty two years ago.

My brother, Nicholas, was two years younger than me, thin, and always changing his hairstyle and clothes. He was grave about his physical appearance, attempted to be a "rock n' roller," and always stole my favorite band t-shirts. His hairstyle was consistently changing from brown to black, or even to pink and blue. It was obvious to the world that he was trying to find himself, but just having a hard time doing it. He was mean most of the time, and we consistently fought like bats out of hell. It was always a race to see who could get the other one in trouble first, yet at the same time, we had each other's backs and everyone knew it.

Majoring in Motherhood

Ryan, my youngest brother, was round faced and round bodied, and he exhibited a huge fascination for building things. I saw him as a pest most of the time, but that was to be expected of an eight year old brother. He was actually rather smart and could hold a solid conversation about mechanics that was well beyond his years. He had the capacity of becoming an inventor, or a world famous engineer.

I was not too tall myself, a rather thin girl with long blonde hair, baby blues, and an impulsive personality. I had always wondered where my blonde hair had come from since the rest of my family had dark hair, but I didn't care enough to question it. I didn't have much confidence socially, but I had plenty of confidence athletically. I was a sorely sarcastic sixteen year old, and life through my eyes was just plain miserable, as I didn't have enough ways to waste my time.

We were currently living in a small southern town in Mississippi, just south of Memphis, a place where everyone knew each other. The weather was always unpredictable, as one day it might storm and then the next day would be as bright as an egg sunny-side up. I had such a strong fascination for weather, and eagerly studied about tornadoes. I was a certified storm spotter by the *National Weather Association*, but had yet to use my newly learned talents. I had a plan to one day become a storm chaser, so

Majoring in Motherhood

long as the tornado didn't swallow me whole first, and I was always keen on watching the sky for strange weather conditions.

I was a strong supporter of most animal activist groups, and I donated to them when I had the money, which was hardly ever. My favorite animal was the killer whale, and I aspired to open up a marine mammal rescue somewhere on the coast one day. I had always had this huge love for whales, dolphins, manatees; you name it, and provided with the right resources, I knew I could start a successful rescue group. With nothing to do on most days, I had plenty of spare time to conduct these magnificent ideas in my head. Hopefully, they would get me somewhere in life.

Majoring in Motherhood

Chapter Two
CJ

    The winter of 2006 was cold and harsh. A thick sheet of snow blanketed the ground, and the weather stayed overcast and rainy. Although the snow was beautiful, I hated that arctic season with a passion. It always caused a layer of ice to form over our driveway, and I was Queen for slipping and falling on it every single year. I also had a grudge on the cold weather, because it was nearly painful to be outside for more than twenty minutes. Your fingers would get so cold that they would go numb, and the air was so nippy that you could barely catch a breath without getting a killer headache. Even though it had only begun, I was more than ready to kiss winter goodbye.

    A few days before Christmas, I finally found that one friend that I had been searching for. However, it was not in human form; my friend came in the form of a horse. He was a beautiful glossy white stallion with crystal blue eyes and powerful muscles that rippled all over his chest and back end. His mane and tail were of the most beautiful cream color, and hung long over his strong, magnificent shape. It was almost like he could have disappeared into the Christmas weather, being the stunning shade of white

Majoring in Motherhood

that he was.

As I watched the horse prance proudly through the snowy pasture, he took on the aura of a unicorn out of a fairytale, only missing his magical horn. He galloped across the field with his tail flying high in the air, reminding me of Gandalf's noble horse, Shadow fax, from *Lord of the Rings*. The horse was so enchanting that it was nearly impossible to keep my eyes off of him. With the way the dim sunlight was shining against him, it was almost as though he was glowing like an angel in the snow.

"He's beautiful," I gushed. I looked up at my father, who was standing beside me.

"Yes, he is, but there is a lot you have to think about," he replied. This would not have been my first, second, or even third horse. In fact, this would have been my thirtieth horse. My family was well seasoned with horses, and we bought horses all the time, trained them, and sold them to eager families. I always smiled when I saw a happy family that had finally found their dream horse, but I had yet to meet the horse that was *my* dream horse...until now.

A few minutes later, the owner of the horse walked over to the fence line.

"Are you folks here to see the horses that I have for sale?" he asked. He was bundled tightly in a thick coat, and his fat cheeks were red from the icy wind that was blowing so steadily.

Majoring in Motherhood

"Yes!" I said excitedly.

"Right this way," he gestured. The stout man was clearly a horse trader, and had round pens and pastures stuffed with all different breeds and colors of horses. There were fat horses, skinny horses, tall horses, short horses, young horses, and old horses, but none of them compared to the white horse that I had first laid my eyes on.

"Is that horse for sale?" I asked. I pointed to the sleek white horse that was standing in the snow.

"Yes, of course! They all are!" chuckled the horse trader.

"Is it a mare?" asked my father. He wasn't too fond of mares, because it grossed him out when they went into heat, and frankly, I couldn't blame him.

"Nope. That there is a stallion," slurred the horse trader. My guess was that he probably hadn't completed high school, considering that this *was* Mississippi.

"Alright then, let's see him," replied Dad. I was so happy to hear my father say those words that I swear my heart smiled at that moment.

The horse trader grabbed a dirty red halter out of his barn, and trudged through the snow toward the white stallion. The horse nickered loudly when he saw the man, and came trotting over to him. After he had buckled the halter on the horse, he opened the gate, and lead him out of the slushy pasture. The melting snow had turned the

Majoring in Motherhood

ground into frosty mud, and the horse and man nearly slipped as they walked toward us.

"Wow, he is beautiful!" I shrieked. I ran to the horse's side, and began rubbing his neck with my hand. His fur was incredibly soft.

"He's a two year old American Quarter Horse, but he's not broke yet," said the horse trader.

"I can do that," I said assertively to my father. I looked over at him with a huge grin on my face, but he didn't return such excitement.

"It's a lot to think about," he said.

"I know it is, but I can do it," I replied readily, "I've done this so many times already." I was beginning to realize how those eager families felt when they'd finally found their dream horse.

"Please! You know I can handle this!" I begged excitedly.

I knew this was the friend that I had needed for so long, and by the friendly way the horse nudged me, I think he might have thought the same thing. I knew my father was right, and that trying to break a horse like this was going to be difficult, but I just couldn't let anything stand between me and my dream horse. I had finally found him, and he was standing right before me.

For a moment, I thought I was never going to own that beautiful animal, because my dad shook his head and

Majoring in Motherhood

retreated back toward the truck. As my heart was sinking, I quickly prayed to God that he would change my father's heart about the situation, because I *had* to have this horse. I needed a hobby and friend so badly at that time in my life.

A few seconds later, my dad turned around, and walked back toward me. "Are you going to pay me back, including a twenty percent interest?" asked my dad.

"Yes!" I shrieked.

"Are you going to wake up early and feed him, as well as our other horses every morning?"

"Yes!"

"Are you going to pay for all his vet bills and keep up with his medical records?"

"Yes!"

"Load him up," said my father to the horse trader.

I was so happy that I could feel my eyes getting blurry with tears of joy. I felt like I had just witnessed a miracle by the way my father had so quickly changed his mind. I gave him a huge hug, and climbed into the back seat of his pickup truck. I was overwhelmingly excited, for all I could see was a bright new future for a special horse and the lucky girl who owned him.

I named my new horse, "CJ," which was short for his registered name, Cactus Jack. He got super lucky, because my dad almost forced me to name him "Tightie Whities," after I battled coming up with a name for him the entire

Majoring in Motherhood

ride home. I couldn't have imagined how embarrassing it would have been to hear at a rodeo, "and here comes Tightie Whities ridden by Barbra Roylance!" Thank God I had quickly thought of the name, CJ.

CJ turned out to be much more than I had bargained for, in fact, CJ turned out to be the worst horse that I had ever owned in my entire life. As a two year old stud, he had a sly personality, and you never knew what stunt he was going to pull next. I was continually getting bucked off right and left, but that didn't stop me from trying to break him into a good riding horse. For some odd reason, I began to enjoy the thrill of riding out his unpredictable behavior, even if it did put me in the hospital a time or two.

One morning around four o'clock, I decided to take CJ for an early morning ride. I couldn't sleep and I had a few hours left, before it was time for school. CJ was acting immensely skittish and I should have taken the hint, but I saddled him up anyway.

"What's the matter, boy?" I asked. He was stomping his foot aggressively, as I tightened the saddle up.

"It's okay," I said soothingly. I rubbed his neck, and climbed into the saddle.

CJ began prancing all over the place, and became uncontrollably anxious. His nostrils were flared, ears alert, and every tiny sound caused him to panic. I sat on his back, trying to calm him, as I watched the sun slowly begin

Majoring in Motherhood

to rise over the pine trees in the distance. Suddenly, CJ became aggressive towards me, and I had to dismount out of the saddle.

"What's the matter with you?" I asked.

I gathered the reins in my hands, and began leading him back to the stable to remove all the riding gear. Just before I was about to tie CJ to the post and take the saddle off, he neighed loudly and reared straight up into the air. Before I could get out of the way, his front hooves hit me on top of the head, and knocked me to the ground full force. Needless to say, I completely passed out. When I awoke a few minutes later, I had a painful headache, and I was so dizzy that it felt like my entire body was spinning in circles.

I forced myself to get off the ground, and found CJ running the fence line like a crazy idiot, and bucking furiously. As I began to come back to my senses, I gathered enough energy to catch CJ, yell obscenities at him, and put him back into his stall. I filled his bucket with water, fed him, and made the long dreary walk to back to my house. When I got home, I found it necessary to wake my parents, because my headache and dizziness were causing me extreme discomfort, and I couldn't see straight. They were anything but pleased.

"What is the matter with you?" snapped Mom. She was completely dumbfounded that I had attempted to ride my stallion that early in the morning.

Majoring in Motherhood

"I'm sorry."
"You could have been killed. You know that horse isn't trustworthy."
"I know I'm sorry," I said.
Two hours later, I found myself in the hospital, where they performed cat scans and x-rays. After sitting there all afternoon, I was finally released from the hospital just fine with nothing other than some expected bruising. Everyone was shocked that I wasn't seriously injured from a twelve hundred pound animal coming down on my head, and advised me to be more cautious.
"Next time, you won't be so lucky," Mom warned.
Apparently, Dad didn't think so either, because the very next day, he had CJ castrated, while I was hanging out with some friends. I was terribly upset when I figured out that my stallion was no longer a stallion, because I had always imagined what a fine breeding stud he could have become. He would have made some beautiful babies. I was angry at my father for gelding my horse without talking to me about it first, but I know he only did it for my safety. I related this to other things my father had done including making me get rid of any animal I brought home whether it was stray dogs, cats, birds, goats, cows, rabbits, pigs, lizards, or fish. I even tried to keep a baby deer one time that I had found stranded in our yard. I'm a parent's worst nightmare. I bet I drove my parents crazy trying to keep every animal I

Majoring in Motherhood

found. I guess I was lucky that my father even allowed me to keep CJ after that incident, but I think he was hoping it would keep me out of trouble during my high school years.

My father also decided that it would be in my best interest to send CJ to a professional horse trainer for further training. My dad's trainer, Walter, was a kind hearted black man who had such a passion for horses. He made his money doing what he loved, and had a good reputation around town for his work. He was the type of man who established a relationship with each and every horse that was sent to him, and he was always sad to see them go.

CJ was very high strung, but Walter was able to calm him down enough to show off his best side. Surprisingly, after only a month and a half of training, CJ was allowed to return home with me. He was well mannered for the first week, but after that, he went back to being the same old unreliable horse. He only showed off his best side when Walter rode him, not a measly one hundred pound girl like myself. He was a horse very set in his ways, and he was bound to let no one change who he was deep inside. CJ would reveal his true colors to me when I least expected it, and I ended up on the ground every single time. I was thrown off of that horse more than any other horse I have ever ridden in my entire life, but I never failed to get right back in the saddle. I wasn't going to let anything hold us back.

Majoring in Motherhood

When my father was convinced that I could handle CJ's bipolar mood swings, we began to take trail rides to different places all over the South. It was nice, because I got to spend some one on one time with my dad, and go on adventures every other weekend. Our favorite place to trail ride was at the Chickasaw State Park, where the paths wove through pine trees and big oak trees, and the trails declined into steep creek embankments that were so tall, you couldn't see over them. It made you feel tough when you rode your horse down hills that were nearly vertical, and managed to make it over the rickety bridge that swung back and forth over the river. It was definitely not the place for inexperienced trail riders.

One foggy morning, CJ showed us just how dangerous the trails could be. A bird flew frantically from a tree and out of nowhere, CJ lost his mind. He arched his back and took off bolting up the side of a steep levee, while I tried desperately to control him. I became terrified as CJ denied my commands, and picked up even more speed over the side of the levee. When he finally reached the top, he galloped straight into the tree packed forest. Trees slammed into my knee caps, and branches scraped across my head and neck, as he bucked and reared. The crunching leaves under CJ's hooves startled him even further, and he began spinning wildly in circles.

"Help!" I screamed.

Majoring in Motherhood

"Hold on! I'm coming!" yelled Dad.

He turned his horse toward the forest, and galloped toward CJ. When my dad finally reached me, he jumped off his horse, and ran into the trees to grab CJ.

"Get off!" he screamed.

I jumped off the side of CJ and landed in the dirt, as he continued to spin in circles wildly. It was a miracle that he didn't trample me to death.

CJ began rearing in a chaotic fight against my father, as he tried to lead him out of the forest. I was worried sick that CJ would strike my father with one of his flailing hooves, but my dad continued to fight back against CJ. Finally, CJ timidly submitted to my father.

"Thanks," I said quietly. I looked over at my father who had sweat dripping from his face, and was boiling hot with anger. He hated CJ.

"Get back on him," Dad demanded. We were two miles from our truck, and there was no way that I could walk CJ that far down all the steep hills. I would have to ride. I trembled as I climbed back into the saddle, while my father held CJ still. He pranced around actively, but I held him steady. I could *not* let that happen again.

"I don't know why you like that crazy animal so much," scolded my father. He sneered at CJ, before climbing back on his horse, Nitro.

"I just do, and he's only two years old. He's still a baby,"

Majoring in Motherhood

I replied.
"Well, is it worth getting killed on him one day?"
"I'll be more careful," I replied firmly.
Dad nodded his head, and pointed in the direction of the trail. "Okay, let's go."
When we were back on the trail, I finally caught a breath of air. My stomach had been in a huge knot, and it felt like I had held my breath for the entire escapade. I fought past my anxiety to keep CJ calm, after I had decided that I wasn't ready to die just yet.

Despite my several close calls on CJ, I still couldn't stop my hungry passion for horses. My father and I continued to take trail rides, and for a while, CJ showed what a remarkable horse he could be. He respected my commands, rode well, and easily loaded up into the horse trailer when it was time for another ride. In fact, he even began to impress my father.

After our fear and fun with trail rides, CJ and I began to venture into the world of hunter jumper. It's an elite sport that tests the teamwork between a horse and rider over an obstacle course of jumps. I saved up money and bought riding breeches, half chaps, boots, a helmet, the proper bit and bridle for CJ, and an English saddle. I even built jumps out in the pasture for CJ and I to practice daily on. I was dedicated to teaching CJ how to compete in hunter jumper, and after a while, he learned exactly what to do.

Majoring in Motherhood

When my parents saw how motivated I was, they began to pay for hunter jumper lessons from a local trainer. Within months, CJ and I had improved, and we were in the show ring. We did our first show at the Alderwood Schooling Show in Germantown, Tennessee, and even though we got last place in all of our classes, I still went home happy as a lark, because CJ had been such a good team mate.

We found out that the girl who got first place in all of our classes happened to be the younger sister of the judge, and we became tuned in on just how rigged all of the competitions were. I learned how tightly knit the community of hunter jumper was, and how everyone knew each other and all of their business. After my father realized this too, he showed no further interest in jumping, and was not supportive of the new sport. Along with lots of practice and lots of falling off came lots of money, which I didn't have. The sport was extremely exciting, but outrageously expensive. Along with that, CJ was not the super tall, lean thoroughbred that the sport beckoned for, so we called it quits.

With nothing better to do on most weekends, I would beg my father to take CJ and I to cheap, saddle club horse shows where we could establish a nice stack of ribbons. I'm talking about the kind of "clearance rack" horse shows where all the old men from town would sit on the

Majoring in Motherhood

bleachers, sip cold beer, and scope out all the young girls on horses. They would yell obnoxiously for the horse that they wanted to win, and gamble for who would take first place.

CJ had a solid conformation of muscles everywhere, which won him first place in almost all halter classes. I also loved entering him in all the speed events, because we loved to go fast. We even chanced barrel racing a few times, and surprisingly, CJ was not that bad. We won some money competing together, and CJ and I even got our names in the local paper for winning third place in 4-D barrels at a competition. I grinned like a five year old on Christmas when I saw it.

Chapter Three
A Typical Teenager

After five long years of homeschooling, I was ready to give public school another go. Sitting at home with your parents day after day isn't exactly what every teenager dreams about. My parents were adamantly against the idea, but after enough arguing and fighting, they unhappily enrolled me into the local public school. At that point, I think they were pretty much ready to just be done with me, because I had caused so much tension in the family. Unfortunately, school that year turned out to be exactly what my parents had predicted it to be.

Every morning at five fifteen, my obnoxiously loud alarm clock would scare me out of my bed, and that's where my day would begin. I would stumble down the stairs, get something to drink, and then jump in the freezing cold shower. Because my parents refused to let me drive, mostly because of the family tension, I had to be at the street by six o'clock to be sure I didn't miss the bus. You can bet I felt cool every morning getting off that banana yellow bus, while all the other kids showed up in their forty thousand dollar sports cars.

I went for weeks without any friends at school, and

Majoring in Motherhood

always hung around by myself. My high school was pretty much a replica of the stereotyped schools you see in movies, because everyone was broken up into different cliques, or groups. You had the upper class "preppy chicks," which hung around the lobby in between classes, and acted like they were the "Queen Bees." Unfortunately, most of them were hideously ugly, and only fit into the group, because they had barely made the cheerleading team, or had daddies made of money. Hanging around in the hallways, you normally found the lower class "stoners" who were always high, always pulling pranks, and always late for class, if they didn't just skip school all together. In the cafeteria, you usually found the two segregated groups of redneck kids and gangster kids. I was on the cross-country team, and you should have found me in the gym with the other athletes from the sports teams, but instead, you found me outside. I enjoyed the peace of being alone, and I didn't want to be associated with any of the different cliques. I just wanted to be myself.

After a few more weeks at school, I finally made friends with a girl named Darby. I was at the Friday night football game with my brother, and she casually walked up, and introduced herself to me. I had been lingering around a skater boy that I had my eye on, and I'm pretty sure that she had noticed. She was a short girl with long curly hair the color of coal, and was part of the stoners group. Although I

Majoring in Motherhood

would have preferred not to be associated with them, I was more than happy to have made a friend, and hung out with the group daily. As expected, I became a "stoner kid," but minus the drugs and weed. I skipped school, failed tests, started smoking cigarettes, and dated some real "winners," if you get what I mean.

Darby was in my State Studies class, and we would continuously harass our teacher, Mr. Mitchell. He would be trying to lecture on some boring state laws that were passed, and Darby and I would slide our shoes across the floor, making loud screeching sounds. He would turn red, his eyes narrowing, and look around the room for the person who had caused a distraction.

Mr. Mitchell loved throwing people out of his class, almost as much as he loved to eat. He was a fat man with a gut that hung jiggling over his size-too-small pants, like the Jell-O that kids played with out of their school lunches. He had a bald head that was so shiny, you could see yourself in it. His wife probably put her make-up on in front of his head every morning. Hey, it saves money, if you don't have to buy a mirror!

His glasses and long scruffy beard made me wonder if he was a wizard, and concocted magical spells in his free time. He was always quite the teacher, using such a mellow toned voice the whole class period, and only ever expressing himself with his hands. It was so easy to lose

Majoring in Motherhood

concentration in his class, and I was always happy when the bell rang.

Darby and I began to spend all our time together, and we became best friends. My friend, Jared, who was also in our State Studies class, unintentionally gave us the nickname of "Darbra." He was running through the halls looking for me one afternoon, and by accident, called out, "Darbra!" Darby and I both turned around with confused faces, as Jared ran down the hall to us.

"I'm sorry, I meant Barbra," he apologized.

"It's okay," Darby said. She had this sarcastic look on her face, and suddenly burst out laughing hysterically.

"What is so funny?" I asked.

"Darbra! Ha ha! It's like we have morphed into one person!" Darby laughed. I couldn't help but laugh with her, which triggered Jared to start laughing too. A teacher stepped out into the hall way, and rudely told us to be quiet.

"Sorry," I giggled.

"This will become the most infamous nickname," said Jared. I didn't actually expect Jared to initiate the trend of calling us that, but he did, and by the end of the week, almost everyone was referring to us as, "Darbra," because we were always together.

Darby and I remained friends for all our high school years, but it seemed like when I needed her the most, she just wasn't there. Like the time that I had a plot to put red

Majoring in Motherhood

food coloring in the seat of Taylor Suggs. Yuck, even her name just makes me want to barf. She was one of the hardest girls to get along with, impeccably conceited, and today, she was wearing skin tight white jeans. I just couldn't resist myself.

Darby and I planned to skip class, and walk to her house to grab the red food dye. Then, during the break between classes, we would squirt just enough red food dye in Taylor's seat to soak through her white jeans, and everyone would think she had started her period. It would be the perfect prank to pull on someone who treated us so unkindly, and it would be hysterically funny. Yes, it was mean, but no one is perfect.

"Okay, we have to sneak out of school to get the dye," I said.

"Got it," replied Darby. She was just as excited about our glorious plan as I was.

"Will you cover for us?" I asked Katie. She was Darby and I's closest friend, and a total member of our group. I always had a feeling that I could never trust Katie, but I didn't care. When you don't have a lot of friends, you have to work with what you've got.

"Yeah, sure," said Katie.

"Okay, let's go!"

As Darby and I snuck out of school to get the red dye, Katie quickly spread the word of our perfect prank. Some

Majoring in Motherhood

friend she turned out to be! By the time we returned to school, Taylor had received the news, and was waiting for us with a group of her friends.

"Did you really think your little friend wouldn't tell me?" asked Taylor. I stared her down, as she continued to rant and rave about how she was so much better than I was. Finally, I had heard enough.

"Would you just shut up?!" I screamed. "Maybe if you were a nicer person I wouldn't be so tempted to make you look like a fool!"

"Fight me!" Taylor yelled. She fisted her hands, and walked straight up to me.

Quickly, a huge group of kids made a circle around us, and started chanting. I turned around to find Darby running away at a million miles an hour. See what I'm talking about? She throws me under the bus just when I need her!

Luckily, a teacher heard about the fight, and stepped outside to break it up.

"Get to class!" the teacher screamed. She was not about to take no for an answer.

I booked it to class as fast as I could, although Taylor had already beaten me there, and the teacher was well aware of what had happened. Needless to say, I was kicked out of class for the day.

Later that day, I finally found Darby.

"Why did you split?" I asked.

Majoring in Motherhood

"I didn't want to get my ass beat."

"Yeah, but you completely ditched me!" I said.

"I know, dude, I'm sorry," Darby moaned. It was obvious that she wasn't proud about being such a chicken.

"We could have won, though, Darby!"

"I know, but I wimped out. Forgive me?"

"Yeah, we're cool." I replied hesitantly.

That wasn't the last time I got in trouble that year, either. The school year consisted of detentions, absences, tardies, failed tests, missing homework, parent teacher conferences, and lots of sneaking out. I think my parents were scared to death about what I would do next, because they installed key loggers onto my computer, and routinely confiscated my cell phone to go through my text messages and phone calls. I felt suffocated without any privacy, and I started smoking to alleviate some of the stress. Late at night, I would climb out my window onto the roof, and smoke cigarettes. My parents would have killed me had they known that I was up on the roof smoking, but they never found out. Well, I guess they did now. Sorry, Mom and Dad!

As I expected, my parents thought I was going out of control, and returned me to homeschooling the following year. As much as I wanted to argue against them, I couldn't, because they were completely right about this one. I definitely deserved to be homeschooled once again.

Chapter Four
A Change of Heart

At seventeen, I sported my first tattoo of a barbed wire heart on my left foot. We had been vacationing over the summer in Destin, Florida, and after several weeks of pleading with my dad, I was finally able to convince him to let me get a tattoo at the local beach shop. Momma was completely against the idea of a tattoo, but since there was no stopping me, she had actually picked out the tattoo herself. My family had nicknamed me, "Barbed Wire," for my cold personality toward them, which was why my mother chose that specific tattoo.

"Prop your foot here," said the tattoo artist. She had short brown hair with black and blonde highlights, and tattoos covered her entire body. She had a very distinct British accent, and had moved from England to open up a tattoo shop with her father.

"Okay," I replied. I sat down, and propped my foot up on the pedestal.

"Is this going to hurt pretty badly?" I asked. The tattoo artist looked down at my thin foot, and nodded her head.

"Well, it certainly isn't going to feel like rainbows and butterflies," she said.

Majoring in Motherhood

I winced, as I heard the buzzing from the tattoo gun. She hadn't even touched my skin yet, and I was already clamming up.

"Look, do you want this tattoo or not?" asked the tattoo artist. She had an irritated tone in her voice.

"Yeah."

"Then stop being a bloody wimp, and give me your foot. I don't have time to play around all day."

"Sorry," I stammered.

"I'm sure you've been quite the bitch to your mother, haven't you?" she asked.

"Ummm..." I was confused. Where did that come from?

"Well, this is for all the times you were a snobby bitch!"

At that moment, the tattoo artist grabbed my foot, and stabbed me with the tattoo gun. I was shocked! Did she really just do that? I watched, as she began to outline my tattoo. I looked up at Mom who was laughing so hard that she could barely stand up. She was tickled to death. I couldn't help but laugh with her, and I didn't squirm even a single time during the whole tattoo.

When it was finished, I was eager to see it. I walked over to a mirror, and examined my foot. It was magnificent! Momma could not have picked a better tattoo for me, and the tattoo artist could not have done a better job. Her undisputable temper had been the bright side of

Majoring in Motherhood

my day, and I was walking out of her shop with a very well done tattoo.

"Thanks so much!" I said excitedly, as I handed her a tip.

"No problem," smiled the tattoo artist. *"Whoa, back up, did she just...smile?"* I thought.

Regardless of Mom's hate for tattoos, she even liked it, and had enjoyed watching the entire procedure. I leaned over, and gave her a hug. She was a good mom, even if we did have a lot of fights.

Around the same time, I began dating the boy that would change my world forever. His name was Erik, and he was a squirrelly looking boy with sandy blonde hair and blue eyes. I knew him through school, but I mostly just avoided him, because he was tremendously annoying. He was always trying to walk me to my classes, and writing me cheesy notes to ask me out.

I don't know what changed inside me that decided to give him a shot, but for whatever the reason, I did. It was definitely a bad decision on my part, but it would take me over a year to realize that. Even though I was being homeschooled again, I still attended most of the Friday night football games, which is where our story began.

It was late fall, and all the leaves were scattering across the football field in shades of red, orange, and yellow. It was a beautiful sight to see, but I was too busy cutting up

Majoring in Motherhood

with Darby and Katie to even notice.

"Hey, what's the score?" someone asked me.

"The heck if I know!" I laughed. I had never really paid much attention to what was going on in the games, only what was going on around them. Our high school had always beaten everyone, except for one exceptionally talented team called South Panola. That is the only game of the year I would watch, and normally, it was completely sold out, and you had to sneak in. Their football players were double the size of ours, and nearly creamed us in every game. It was certainly a game you didn't want to miss.

"We are leaving," said Darby.

"What, why?" I complained. I wasn't ready to leave the game yet.

"We are going to hang out at Justin's house." *"Oh, that's why she's leaving,"* I thought. Darby had been exceedingly interested in this guy for a while, even though she already had a boyfriend, and he was finally starting to make a move on her.

"Well, okay, have fun," I said.

"Come with us!" she yelled. The high school bands were now playing, and it was nearly impossible to hear anything over the explosively loud music.

"No thanks!" I screamed. I didn't feel like getting into any trouble that night, and I knew if I went with her, I

Majoring in Motherhood

would get into trouble. I waved to Darby, and sat down against the fence line. *"Great, my friends left,"* I thought. This night was getting more and more boring.

Out of the corner of my eye, I saw Erik headed my way. *"Oh no,"* I thought, *"go the other way!"* However, Erik was headed right in my direction.

"You mind if I sit next to you?" he asked. I wanted to say no. He had asked me out so many other times, and I knew that's what he was after. He was so desperate.

"Sure."

He sat down, and leaned against the fence. My eyes were watering from how cold it was, and I was trying to keep my composure. The cold wind blew across my face, sending shivers down my spine, and turning my nose bright red. Oh, why hadn't I brought a warmer jacket?

"Are you cold?" asked Erik. He motioned for my hand.

"A little," I said, as I allowed him to take it. *"What am I doing? I can't stand this guy,"* I thought. He wrapped my hands inside his warm hoodie, and soon, I was able to feel the blood run back into my fingers.

"So, how have you been?" he asked.

"I'm good. My friends left, but I wasn't ready to go yet." He stared right into my eyes as I spoke, which made me a little uncomfortable.

"Oh, I'm sorry," he replied. "Well, we should hang out sometime." I could tell he was really hoping I would yes.

Majoring in Motherhood

"Okay, sure." I shivered again.

"You're still cold. Here let me help." Erik wrapped his arms around me, and his thick hoodie blocked out most of the freezing cold wind. I couldn't help but smile.

"I know you hate me, but umm..."

"Will I go out with you?" I asked.

Erik smiled. "Yeah, that!"

I lingered on the subject for a minute. Did I really want to go out with this guy? Then, I had a change of heart.

"I'll give you one chance," I said.

Just then, Darby and the rest of my friends ran up behind us, and grabbed us through the chain link fence. I nearly felt my heart jump out of my body.

"What the hell is this!" yelled Darby. She had a sarcastic grin on her face, and stared at Erik's arm around me. She was stoned out of her mind.

"Nothing," I said.

"Are you really going out with this freak?" she asked. Erik shot Darby a death glare, but he knew she was just kidding. They were good friends.

"Yes, she is," said Erik. He smiled at me. *"Maybe this won't be so bad,"* I thought to myself, but then again, only time would tell.

At the end of the football game, Erik and I were still huddled up together on the fence line. I didn't want to leave. I was so comfortable, and thoroughly enjoying this

Majoring in Motherhood

snuggling. It was keeping me warm. My phone started vibrating in my pocket, and I reached for it. It was my mother.

"Hello?" I asked, even though I full well knew who it was.

"Do you need me to pick you up?" asked Mom.

"No, Darby is giving me a ride home."

"Okay, well you need to come straight home. You're still grounded."

"Ugh...Okay," I said as I hung up the phone. I looked over at Erik.

"Sorry, but I have to go. I'm kind of grounded."

"Okay, you need a ride?" asked Erik.

"No, that's okay. Darby is giving me one."

I gave Erik my number, and he promised to text me later that night. He wrapped his arms around me, and hugged me tightly.

"Goodnight," he smirked.

"Goodnight," I gushed.

On the ride home, Darby quizzed me like crazy.

"So, you're going out with Erik now?" she asked.

"Maybe."

"Why?" Darby asked, "I thought you hated his guts."

"Well, I did."

"So, what, now you don't?"

"I'm not sure," I responded. I didn't quite know what I

Majoring in Motherhood

was getting myself into. I looked over at Darby who had another sarcastic look on her face. I started to wonder, if she was slightly jealous of me dating Erik.

"Will you spend the night at my house tomorrow?" Darby asked.

"I'll ask Momma," I replied.

"We have things to talk about!"

"I know, I know," I said, "I have to go inside, I'll see you tomorrow."

Darby dropped me off at the street, and I made the long walk up our winding driveway. I hummed quietly, as I thought about Erik. I wasn't going to tell my parents. Mom was waiting for me, when I walked in the door.

"How was the game?"

"Good."

"What was the score?" she asked. *"Oh, great,"* I thought, *"the one damn time I don't know the score."*

"Umm... 13 to 5?" I tried. I honestly had no clue.

"No, it wasn't," Mom paused, "Did you even go to the game, Barbra?" Her face was serious.

"Of course I did! I'm not going to lie about that. I just wasn't paying attention."

"Okay, do not disappoint me," said Mom.

"I love you."

"I love you too," I replied.

I walked upstairs to my bedroom, and collapsed on my

Majoring in Motherhood

bed. I had a bad feeling in my heart about dating Erik, but for some reason, I just ignored it. Not to mention, I felt bad for not telling my parents about my new boyfriend. I closed my eyes, and thought about everything. I knew there was something not right about the situation, but I wasn't about to give up on Erik yet. That would come much later.

Later that night, Erik finally texted me. I had been waiting for a couple hours, and I was constantly checking my phone every few minutes, just in case I hadn't heard it vibrate.

The text read," hey beautiful." I felt myself blush.

We stayed up all night chatting, and I slowly started to fall for Erik. I didn't really know what it was that I saw in him, but there was something that I liked. Maybe it was the sweet nothings he had said to me that night? Or maybe I was just having a change of heart?

Majoring in Motherhood

<u>Chapter Five</u>
What is love, anyway?

The following night, I spent the night at Darby's house. It took a lot of work to get my parents to agree, but after about five hours of sweet talking, and then massively cleaning my disastrous bedroom, I finally got the okay. Once I got there, Darby called Erik to see if he wanted to hang out with us.

"Hello?" Erik answered.

"Hey dude! It's Darby. What's up?"

"Just chilling," responded Erik, "You?"

"Not much, I'm good. Anyways, Barbra is at my house, so you should come over!"

"Really? Sweet! I'm only three apartments down. Meet me at the playground?" Erik asked. There was a playground built inside the apartment complex about a quarter mile up the street.

"Sure," said Darby. She hung up the phone, and looked over at me. I was all smiles.

"Well, aren't you Miss Happy?"

"Yes," I replied. It was true. I was super excited to see him again.

Even though it was almost midnight, Darby and I had

Majoring in Motherhood

the freedom to wander around wherever we pleased, because her parents worked all night. They normally didn't return home, until about five o'clock in the morning. I sat down on the couch, and began lacing up my converses, while Darby slipped her flip flops on.

"Will you hurry up? God, you take forever!" she complained.

"Sorry."

"Okay, can we go now?"

"Wait, hold on a second," I said. I ran to the mirror in her bathroom, and lined my eyes in ebony black eyeliner. I thought it looked super sexy.

"Let's go!" Darby yelled. She was growing impatient.

"Gees, woman! I'm coming!" I returned to her waiting out front with the door standing wide open. I could feel the cold air rushing inside her humid apartment. It was another ridiculously frigid night. I pulled the door closed behind me, and we started up the street. It was pitch black outside, regardless of the few flickering street lights that lined the road, and my heart was pounding. What if he didn't like me anymore?

"There he is," pointed Darby. Erik was leaning against his old blue mustang. It was a worn out model from the early 90's, but he still looked good against it. I walked up to Erik, and gave him a flirty smile.

"Hey," I said sheepishly.

Majoring in Motherhood

"Hey," he replied.

"Well, while you two love birds chat, I'm going to swing!" yelled Darby. We followed her over to the playground, where Erik and I stood underneath the slide, and talked.

"You look so good," said Erik. I blushed. I wasn't used to all these sweet compliments.

"Thanks," I replied.

Suddenly, a car pulled into the apartment complex, and Erik ducked underneath the slide.

"What's going on?" I asked. I watched the car circle around the apartment complex numerous times.

"That's my mom."

"Okay, well, why are you hiding?"

"I'm supposed to be inside with my friend, and she would freak out, if she knew I wasn't there."

"Oh," I responded. I watched Erik's mother drive past his car. She was checking up on Erik to make sure he was where he was supposed to be.

"She looks mean," I said.

"Yeah, she is," replied Erik.

A few minutes later, Erik's mom drove off, and he came out of hiding. It was confusing to me why he felt he had to hide from her, but I didn't say anything about it.

"I better get back to my friend's house," Erik said. "She might come back."

Majoring in Motherhood

"Okay," I replied. I looked over at Erik who was staring at the ground.

"So..."

"Yeah?"

"Are you really my girlfriend?" Erik asked. I stared into his blue eyes for a moment. Was I?

"Yes," I smiled. Erik pulled me close to him, and wrapped his arms around me.

"I have to go," he whispered.

"I know." He squeezed me even tighter, before he let go, and departed.

"Text me!" Erik yelled, as he ran back to his friend's apartment.

I drug my feet over to Darby, who was still swinging.

"You guys are gross," she joked.

"I know, right?" We both laughed like two tickled first graders, before we walked back to her apartment. We stayed up all night talking about boys, before we finally fell asleep at the crack of dawn. About an hour later, Erik called me.

"Hello?" I mumbled. I was so tired that I could barely talk. Sixty minutes is not near enough time to sleep.

"Get up. You're going to church with me," he said.

"What?"

"Get dressed," Erik demanded. I rubbed my eyes for a few seconds. I was craving sleep more than anything, but I

Majoring in Motherhood

wasn't going to turn Erik down the first time he called.

"Give me like fifteen minutes," I groaned. After I got off the phone with Erik, I called my mother's cell phone. I didn't want to wake the entire household this early.

"Mom, can I go to church with a friend?" I asked.
"Who?"
"This guy named Erik." I held my breath.
"Okay, but you have to come home afterwards," Mom replied.

"Yes ma'am." I got off the phone with Momma, and rolled out of bed. I could barely stand up straight, but I managed to make it over to where Darby had fallen asleep.

"Darby," I whispered. No response. I shook her back and forth, until she cracked one eye open.

"What?" she snapped.
"Do you want to go to church with Erik and I?"
"Hell no," Darby groaned. She pulled the covers over her head, and immediately fell back asleep.

"I'll call you," I whispered.

A few minutes later, Erik stopped by to pick me up.

"Good morning!" He sung cheerfully.
"Morning," I replied drowsily.
"You need to wake up," said Erik.
"Well, I only got one hour of sleep."
"I'll fix that," Erik replied. He drove down the street to the nearest drug store, and parked his car.

Majoring in Motherhood

"I'll be right back," he said, as he unbuckled his seat belt. A few minutes later, he came back outside with the biggest can of Red Bull that I have ever seen.

"This should fix you," he said confidently.

"Oh my gosh, I will never be able to drink all that!" I replied. However, within a few minutes, I had downed the entire can, and was as wide awake as the Energizer Bunny.

When we arrived at Erik's church, my whole mood changed. I did not want to be here this early in the morning, and I knew that Erik wasn't here to listen to a good sermon. He was just here to make a statement with me.

As we walked into the church, a million girls immediately ran over to gossip with Erik. They looked me up and down, and casually pushed me out of their way. The swarm of girls attacked Erik like a mob of angry flies attacking a bug lantern, but sadly, none of them were getting zapped to death. They cheaply flirted, not even because they liked Erik, but just because they saw me as fresh meat in their territory. Unfortunate for them, they were hardly threatening, considering that most of them were fat, fake, or just plain ugly.

This was one of the reasons I hated church. It wasn't a place of worship, it was a place to get seen. "*Gross*," I thought, "*deduct point number one*." I hadn't even had time to give this church a chance, and I was already deducting

Majoring in Motherhood

points.

Finally, Erik broke free from the crowd.

"Sorry about that." I nodded my head, as we walked into the main building of the church. It looked to me like the church had wasted thousands of dollars on unnecessary luxury items for the pastor. His seat appeared to be none other than a La-Z-Boy recliner set up behind the oak wood pedestal. Wow, what a way to spend the money of struggling people. They're already in debt, but no worries! We'll just make them feel so guilty that they have to tithe us, and then we'll spend all their hard earned money on a leather recliner!

This was the thing that infuriated me the most, and what I hated so much about churches. They were businesses, rather than a holy place to worship God, and this was why I didn't go to church. I bet the pastor drove a Mercedes Benz, or a Porsche. "*Deduct point number two*," I thought. This church was definitely not on to a good start.

As the pastor walked up to the podium, I knew I was going to have to suffer through the next two hours. The church members shouted and whistled when he entered the room, like he was the new Jesus, or a celebrity. You can bet that I was wishing I hadn't answered my phone that morning, because I was definitely paying the consequences.

The pastor grabbed his microphone, and immediately began his speech filled with sneaky tactics that lead church

Majoring in Motherhood

members to furnish him with more money. His sermon consisted of "give your money back to God, and he will bless you," and "you cannot live a selfish life, and truly be happy." I was barfing on the inside. This guy was ridiculous!

I turned around to find many eyes locked on me. It was mostly all the teenage girls that had hoarded around Erik like buzzards, but also some of the older church women, and the older perverted men. Gosh, you would think that no one new *ever* came into this church. I rolled my eyes, and turned back around. What kind of church was this, anyway? I glanced down at my cell phone to check the time. It had only been forty five minutes, but it felt like hours had passed. The time was surely not flying by like I had hoped it would.

Finally, everyone stood up to sing worship songs. By that time, I knew this torture had to be almost over. It had been over two hours, and my butt was immensely sore from sitting for so long. Everyone threw their arms up in the air, and swayed back and forth to the music, while the overly aged women sang excruciatingly loud. The pastor had his head flung back as far as it could go with his hands lifted up toward the ceiling. I was getting scared for my sanity! I was a Christian by all means, but this seemed more like a gimmick, than a church!

At last, it was all over. The torment had stopped, and

Majoring in Motherhood

we were finally making our way back out to the parking lot. Just as we were about to leave, a few of the jealous teenage girls ran over to talk with Erik again. I was getting agitated beyond all means. This was insane! We had been at the church for over four hours, and I just wanted to leave, so that I could actually *talk* to my new boyfriend! We had hardly spoken a word this entire time.

The girls giggled and touched Erik on the arms, as they made terrible attempts at flirting. "*Okay, I have had ENOUGH,*" I thought. This was ending now. I walked over to Erik, shoving some of the girls out of my way, and shot him a sexy smile.

"Baby," I flirted. Erik looked over at me with a huge grin on his face.

"Let's go ahead and leave," I said, as I motioned to his car.

"Okay, babe," replied Erik. I could tell that he was loving the fact that I called him "baby."

"Nice to meet all of you," I sneered to the group of rude girls, as we got in the car. Score one for me!

On the ride home, Erik and I talked, and slowly got to know each other.

"So, what do you want to do today?" asked Erik. I knew exactly what I wanted to do, and that was to spend some quality time with good ole' CJ. I hadn't ridden him in quite a few days, and he needed a good ride.

Majoring in Motherhood

"Well, I want to go ride CJ," I said. Erik raised his eye brows, and looked at me.

"Ride who?"

"CJ, my horse!" I chimed.

"Uh, I'm not too sure about that. I don't like riding horses," he replied. I could tell he was nervous.

"It's the least you can do for me. I did just sit through four hours of church for you," I smiled. Erik looked at me with a worried expression.

"But, I'm afraid of horses."

"No need to be afraid. CJ loves everyone!" Okay, so I lied. CJ didn't love everyone, in fact, he hated almost everyone he came in contact with.

"Okay, if you're sure," replied Erik.

When we got to my house, my parents were eager to meet the new "friend" of mine. Luckily, Erik was all dressed up in slacks and a shirt, so he looked like a nice guy.

"Hello, I'm Nancy," said Mom. Erik reached out, and shook her hand.

"I'm Erik, it's very nice to meet you," he replied.

"Hello, Mr. Roylance," said Erik.

"Hello," replied Dad. He reached out, and shook Erik's hand a little harder than Momma had.

"Okay, well we are going to ride CJ," I said.

"Alright, be careful," said Momma.

Majoring in Motherhood

"No worries," I replied.

I walked out into the garage, and began loading equipment into the back of my dad's four wheeler.

"Can I help?" asked Erik.

"Yeah, get those brushes and that halter for me," I replied. Erik gathered up the equipment, and lifted it into the back of the four wheeler.

"Thank you," I said.

After I made sure we had everything, I drove up to the horse pasture where CJ was waiting for me. He had his head hung over the fence, and neighed loudly.

"Hi, buddy!" I yelled. I parked the four wheeler, and ran up to the fence to love on CJ. He rested his head on my shoulder, until he saw Erik, and then he nudged me away. He nickered at Erik, who was hidden behind me.

"He wants to meet you," I said. Erik slowly walked toward CJ, and paused.

"I don't know what to do," he said. I grabbed Erik's hand, and pulled him closer to the horse.

"Put your hand out like this," I motioned. I held Erik's hand, and slowly put it on CJ's velvety nose.

"It's so soft," said Erik. I nodded my head. It was true, CJ had a very soft nose. I watched, as Erik continued to stroke his face.

"I think he likes you," I said. Erik smiled. CJ flared his nostrils, and inhaled Erik's scent. It was a horse's way of

Majoring in Motherhood

getting to know someone.

"Okay, let's ride him," I said. CJ must have understood what I said, because by the time I had opened the gate, he was half way across the field. "*Oh, great*," I thought, "*another round of let's chase the stupid horse.*" I walked closer toward CJ with his halter, and he darted in the opposite direction.

"Get over here!" I yelled, as CJ trotted off. He snorted as loud as he could, and flung his head up in the air. He thought he was a real big shot.

Erik laughed hysterically, while I chased CJ all over the pasture for a half hour. However, I think CJ got sick of playing tag, because he finally gave in, and let me catch him.

"You dumb horse," I whispered. He rubbed his face on me, nearly lifting me off the ground.

I walked him back up to the front of the pasture, and tied him to the fence post. CJ was a dusty mess, and had big spots of mud all over his pearly white coat. He turned his head sideways, so that he could watch me, while I walked over to the four wheeler and gathered up all his grooming brushes and combs.

"Hey, boy," said Erik. He walked up to CJ, and pat him on his face, however, CJ didn't return the kind greeting. He threw his head up in the air, knocking Erik to the ground, and causing his nose to bleed.

Majoring in Motherhood

"CJ!" I screamed. I ran over to help Erik up off the ground, and to look at his nose.

"Are you okay?" I asked. Blood was running all down his face, and staining his church shirt.

"I think so," replied Erik. I helped him over to the four wheeler, and sat him down. He tilted his head back, and waited for the bleeding to stop.

"I'm sorry," I said.

"It's okay. I have nose bleeds a lot."

"Oh, well, do you still want to ride him?" I asked.

"Sure."

After Erik's nose had stopped bleeding, and I groomed CJ back into a clean horse, I showed Erik how to saddle him up.

"You put the saddle pad over his withers like this," I said. Erik watched, as I slid the pad over CJ's shoulders, and fit it to him properly.

"Then, you lift the saddle onto his back."

"Okay," replied Erik. He didn't seem to enthralled with the whole "how to saddle a horse up" lesson, but at least he was paying attention.

"After that, we have to tighten up the cinch," I said.

"What's the cinch?" asked Erik. I pointed to the leather strap that was looped around CJ's girth.

"And what's that thing?" asked Erik.

"That's the girth. It goes under their belly, and holds the

Majoring in Motherhood

saddle on their back."

"Oh, okay," replied Erik.

"Here, help me tighten up the saddle," I said. Erik walked to the other side of CJ, and together, we tightened up the cinch, until the saddle was no longer sliding around on CJ's back.

"Thanks," I flirted.

"No problem."

Finally, it was time to ride. I climbed up on CJ, and rode him around the pasture to warm him up. CJ lazily drug his hooves along, and hung his head low.

"Come on, boy, let's go!" I shouted excitedly. CJ immediately perked his ears forward, and lifted his hooves into a fast gallop from a slow walk. I felt proud to have been the one who taught him that. CJ and I paraded all over the pasture in a fierce gallop. I felt the wind rushing through my hair, as CJ continued to pick up speed, and I smiled happily. I was in pure heaven on my horse, and I hoped Erik would enjoy riding CJ, as much as I did.

After a few minutes, I rode CJ back over to the gate where Erik was standing.

"Wow," he said.

"I know. You're going to love it," I replied, as I climbed out of the saddle.

"Yeah, but I don't know about this." Erik didn't even have enough time to finish talking, before I had helped lift

Majoring in Motherhood

him into the saddle.

"I'm not so sure about this," Erik said, as CJ stomped his hoof impatiently.

"You'll be fine," I replied. I hooked a lead rope to CJ's halter, and slowly began to guide him around the pasture.

"See, it's fun," I said to Erik. He smiled at me, and rubbed CJ's shoulder.

After a couple laps around the pasture, I sped CJ up to a trot. Erik bounced around obnoxiously in the saddle.

"This is so bumpy!" Erik yelled, as he held on to the saddle.

"Put all your weight into your heels, and it won't be as bad," I said. Erik nodded his head, and sunk all his weight into his heels. Sure enough, his bumping drastically decreased.

"This is fun," said Erik.

"I told you," I replied. I looked up at Erik, and smiled.

"Can I try to ride him by myself?" I made a weird face, and thought about what the consequences could be. Erik was definitely not ready to ride CJ by himself.

"Are you sure?" I asked.

"Yes," he replied.

"Well, okay," I mumbled.

I unhooked the lead rope from CJ's halter, and stepped aside. As I started walking back toward the gate, CJ turned around, and began to loyally follow me.

Majoring in Motherhood

"He won't listen to me," complained Erik.

"You have to make him. Pull the reins in the direction you want to go, and give him a little kick with your heels."

Erik coaxed CJ in the opposite direction, and CJ sped up into a quick trot. "*Oh, no,*" I thought, "*this isn't going to end well.*" Sure enough, CJ's trot quickly turned into a gallop, as Erik slung back and forth in the saddle.

"Slow down!" I yelled.

"I can't! He won't stop!" Erik shrieked.

I watched as CJ rounded a corner, and continued galloping around the pasture with Erik flailing back and forth on his back.

"Pull back on the reins!" I yelled.

At that moment, I watched the reins fall out of Erik's hands, and CJ began galloping even faster. "*Well, so much for that,*" I thought. I ran right in front of CJ, and held both my hands out. CJ stopped dead in his tracks, nearly sending Erik flying over the top of his head. He was holding onto the saddle horn for dear life, and shaking.

"I want off," Erik said. I helped Erik climb out of the saddle, and hooked the lead rope back to CJ's halter. I tied him to the fence post, and began taking the tack off of him. He was foaming with sweat all over his shoulders and rear end.

"Man, you really got a work out," I joked to CJ. He nuzzled his face into my side, and snorted slobber all over

Majoring in Motherhood

my jeans.

"Thanks," I huffed.

When we got back to the house, my parents asked how riding CJ went.

"Oh, just great," Erik said sarcastically. My dad laughed.

"Well, that's what I expected out of him," he replied. I stared over at my father, who was sitting at the kitchen table with a huge grin wiped across his face. I could tell by his expression that he didn't like Erik.

"CJ ran away with him, and he had a nose bleed," I said. I looked over at Erik's bloody shirt.

"I told you to get rid of that stupid horse," replied Dad. His grin had suddenly turned into a serious expression.

"I know, but I'm just going to keep working with him," I said.

"Yeah, if he doesn't kill you first," said Dad. I hung my head, and stared at the kitchen floor. I knew my father was just trying to prove a point. No matter what anyone else thought, CJ was my horse, and I loved him.

"Do you want some Tylenol?" I asked Erik. He nodded his head, and I unscrewed the cap on the Tylenol bottle.

"I'm sorry about CJ," I said as I reached into the cabinet, and picked up a glass.

"It's okay," Erik replied. I filled the glass with water, and handed it to him, along with the Tylenol. He passed

Majoring in Motherhood

me a small smile, while he leaned his head back, and swallowed the Tylenol. Then, he gulped down the cold water.

"Want to go to my house?" he asked.

"Sure."

Once we got to Erik's house, I met his mother and stepfather, Lisa and Steve, for the first time. Lisa was a short woman with scraggly brown hair, which was styled in the most puzzling way, and worked at a hair salon, while Steve was a tan "biker dude" with a conspicuously nasally voice that worked at an optometrist's office. They were nice, until his mom saw the blood on his shirt, and freaked out.

"What happened to you?" she asked.

"I had another nose bleed."

"Then why didn't you come home, and take some medicine?"

"Because, Barbra gave me some," he replied. Lisa glared over at me, and looked me up and down disapprovingly.

"You know he's allergic to ibuprofen," she barked.

"No, I didn't know that, and I gave him Tylenol," I replied debatably. I was shocked at how quickly Lisa's mood had changed, and how much she treated Erik like a baby. "*I think he's smart enough to know what kind of medicine he can or can't have,*" I thought. I stared at the

Majoring in Motherhood

floor, so that I didn't have to retain eye contact with Erik's parents any longer. It hadn't even been five minutes, and I already disliked them.

Throughout the night, Lisa asked me numerous questions about myself, and made me feel uncomfortable about being in her home. When I was standing up, her husband, Steve, would tell me to sit down, and point to a spot on the couch. However, I didn't want to sit down. I just wanted to go home.

Finally, Erik drove me home, and I was able to relax.

"My parents like you," he said. I rolled my eyes.

"I'm sure they do," I replied. Anyone in their right mind knew that they didn't like me, and it was concrete that I didn't like them either. As we pulled up in my driveway, Erik reached out for my hand slowly.

"I love you," he said. My mind went blank. He loves me? How could he love me, already? Has this guy lost his mind? Yet, something in the back of my mind liked it. It made me feel all warm and fuzzy inside that someone said they loved me.

"Umm...," I said. I didn't really know what to say, because I didn't love him just yet. I mean, we hardly knew each other outside school. Erik was staring right at me, and I felt obligated to say it. I couldn't just leave him hanging like that.

"I love you too," I replied. Erik smiled, and kissed me

Majoring in Motherhood

on the hand.

"I'll see you tomorrow," he said. I nodded my head, and got out of the car. My mind was spinning in wild circles. Was I really about to jump head first into a relationship? I had never even been in a serious relationship before! As I walked inside the house, I knew that I was going to do this no matter what my instincts told me. I was going to commit myself to a relationship for the first time in my young life.

Over the next few months, I spent nearly every day with Erik, and we jumped head first into a wild relationship. We learned pretty much everything about each other; the good, the bad, and the super ugly. Unfortunately, I would have to say that Erik was more of a bad influence on me than a positive reinforcement, because of how deceptive our relationship was. We were constantly fighting and breaking up over lies, but then getting back together the next day, only to do it again. Jealousy overwhelmed our relationship, and the lack of trust caused a lot of friction between us. I realized how quickly Erik's mood changed, just like his mother, and should something upset him, he took out all his anger on me. A simple argument could turn into a physical fight within a moment's notice, and there was nothing I could do to stop it. I should have run for the hills, but with him being my first real relationship, I thought this was just some "tough love."

Majoring in Motherhood

Erik's mother, Lisa, surely didn't make our relationship any easier either, as she was always sticking her nose where it didn't belong. If Erik and I were hanging out on a date, she would blow his phone up, until he finally answered her call. Then, if he didn't tell her exactly what she wanted to hear, she would threaten him by taking things away whether it was his car, his friends, or even me. Sometimes, she would even make us drive out of our way to her hair salon, just so that she could quiz Erik about what we were up to. She would be busy hacking away at someone's hair, and asking Erik and I personal questions right in front of her customers. It was insanely unprofessional. I surely would not have been one to sit in her chair, considering that Lisa was an overly chatty woman who talked with her hands, whether she was holding scissors, or not. I learned just how manipulative Erik's mother was, and how she had this sick obsession with controlling everything in her son's life. Maybe that was the reason Erik was always on edge? Too bad he had been an only son.

My parents had also quickly caught on to the fact that Erik and I were dating, and were highly objective to it. They didn't like Erik, because of the careless way he treated me, his irresponsible ways, and the fact that he always smelled like cigarettes. Erik didn't care that I had sensitive feelings, and pushed me around back and forth, because he

Majoring in Motherhood

knew that he could rein me back in every time with some sympathetic words. Lisa even called me one time just to ask me "what the hell I was doing dating Erik," although I knew it was only another one of her manipulative attempts to break up our relationship. Ever since I had come around, she felt like she was losing her control over Erik, and wanted to "eliminate the problem." However, the more my parents and Erik's parents wanted us separated, the tighter we held on to each other. This was love, and we were in it for the long run, or so I thought.

Majoring in Motherhood

<u>Chapter Six</u>
Something is Different

One of the quirks about homeschooling is that you can finish an entire year's worth of work in a few months, so that's exactly what I did. I graduated early, and fresh out of high school, my parents allowed me to attend the college of my choice, and stay in the dorms. I picked out a community college that was one hour away, because it featured a rodeo team, and I could take CJ with me. I mean, what more could I ask for? I was going to have my beloved horse away at college with me! Not to mention that I had even earned myself a scholarship that covered nearly all of my tuition!

I personally thought CJ was the most beautiful horse on the rodeo team, although he was not the fastest. Most of the horses on the team were extremely high quality barrel racing horses that had thousands of dollars of training installed in them, but CJ was not that type of horse. I didn't have thousands of dollars to spend on his training, and in my opinion, he didn't need it. He was a fine horse just the way he was.

CJ and I carried the American flag in one of the bull riding rodeos our college hosted, and he did an immaculate

Majoring in Motherhood

job. The stands were packed full of excited audience, yet CJ didn't let the screaming crowd frighten him even one time. He paraded around the arena conceitedly, and galloped with our flag flying high. That was one of my fondest memories of CJ. I also remember galloping bareback in the pasture under a cloudless blue sky, and thinking how lucky I was to be a girl enjoying her horse at that moment. I can't explain to you the bond I had with my horse, and nothing could have come between us. I loved waking up at five in the morning to take care of him before my classes, because he would love on my shoulder, and neigh at me for his breakfast. He was my sunshine in a world of rain.

Only being one month into eighteen, the freedom from my parents' wing was just as candy coated as I had imagined it to be. I could do whatever I wanted and whenever I wanted to do it. Later, I would find out that this had been another one of my parents' secret attempts to end my relationship with Erik, but if only they had been successful. Erik and I continued to see each other and our relationship became more serious than ever.

Over the next semester, life became more difficult than I could have ever anticipated. One of my best friends, Neal, got into some serious trouble that almost turned my life upside down. He made threats about killing the president over the internet, and his nasty ex-girlfriend, Amanda, sold

Majoring in Motherhood

him out. She called the police, and within hours, a huge investigation was opened up. When Neal heard that homeland security was coming after him, he panicked, and fled. He disappeared for an entire week, and I was the only person in the world who knew exactly where he was.

Secret Service was sent out to question me about my friendship with Neal, but I lied about everything. I didn't want to be involved in a case like this, and I was worried about what they might do to him. They tapped my phone calls, hacked my email accounts, and tore apart my Facebook and MySpace accounts looking for information, but found nothing. Wherever I went, there was a secret service agent trailing not far behind me. They knew that I was lying about Neal's whereabouts, but I was just a step ahead of them. They weren't going to get any information out of me.

Secret Service followed me around for days, and it became nearly impossible to concentrate on my class work. My grades began to slip, and soon, I realized just how serious this dilemma was. I turned on the television one night, only to find that Neal's case had made the news report, and my name was being slandered in newspaper columns and online articles! I could go to jail for keeping information from the government! Finally, I snapped. I told everyone where Neal was located, and a warrant was sent out for his arrest.

Majoring in Motherhood

Neal was located within twenty four hours, and thrown into federal prison with many charges against him. I wrote letters to him for months, while he was in prison, until he became ill minded. He began sending me frightening letters that emphasized his murderous rage toward everyone, and what he wanted to do to them in sickening detail. I became uncomfortable about the situation, and slowly stopped replying to Neal's treacherous letters. A year later, he was released from prison, and wrote me one final letter that elucidated my betrayal to him and his sincere hate for me. Conclusively, that was the last time I ever heard from Neal.

Erik and I continued to fight, which caused my life to become even more stressful than it already was, but for some reason, I just couldn't pull away from him. It was like I was drawn to him, and no matter how hard I tried, I couldn't allow myself to break free of his chains. He would ridicule me, deceive me, and see other girls outside of our relationship, which cause me to feel insecure. I felt God speaking to my heart about the situation, but I just wasn't ready to let Him take hold of my life yet. I was too sucked in to the Devil's foreplay with Erik and I's relationship. I allowed him to make me feel uncomfortable in my own skin, and consequently, I started abusing diet pills to lose weight, as well as other unhealthy eating habits. It went on for a couple of weeks, until I started realizing that

Majoring in Motherhood

something was going on with my body, something that would change my life forever.

Majoring in Motherhood

Chapter Seven
What do we do now?

"I can't do this," I said. I stared over at Alyssia, who was standing next to me. She was my best friend at college, and had always had my back no matter what.

"You have to," she replied.

"Nope, not doing it."

"Okay, then I'll do it," Alyssia said. She walked over to the aisle where the pregnancy tests were, and began reading the backs of the boxes.

"Alyssia, what if someone sees us?"

"Look, do you want to know, or not?" she asked.

"I want to know."

"Okay, then suck it up, and get over here!" she yelled. I nodded my head, and slowly drug my feet over to the pregnancy test aisle. There were so many different kinds to choose from, and the more I looked at them, the sicker I felt.

"Just grab one," I said.

"Are you sure?"

"Yes. I can't stand here any longer."

Alyssia grabbed the pregnancy test that was the closest to her, and we made our way to the cash register. I stared

Majoring in Motherhood

at the floor, as Alyssia handed it to the old lady behind the counter. She glared meanly at us, as she rang up the pregnancy test, and put it into a plastic bag. We payed for the test, and quickly made our way back to the dorms.

"It's now or never," said Alyssia. She opened up the box, and pulled out the pregnancy test.

"Go on," she said, as she handed me the test.

"Okay," I mumbled. I locked myself into a bathroom stall, and stared at the pregnancy test. I didn't want to take it. I just wanted to close my eyes, and make everything disappear. I was only eighteen! I shouldn't be taking a pregnancy test yet!

Finally, I closed my eyes, and took the test. I told myself there was nothing to worry about, and everything would be just fine. As I opened my eyes, I felt my heart drop into my stomach, as an undeniable plus sign showed up in the results window. This couldn't be happening to me! My parents would kill me in my sleep, if they found out!

"Well, what's the results?" asked Alyssia. I felt myself go numb, as I walked out of the bathroom stall. Alyssia stared at my trembling body, and her mouth dropped.

"No way," she said. I handed her the pregnancy test, and walked over to the sinks in the bathroom. I washed my hands and paused for a minute, as I looked at myself in the mirror. *"God, why did you choose me to be a mother?"* I

Majoring in Motherhood

thought. I waited a few seconds for an answer, before I turned around.

"You're going to be a mom," Alyssia said.

"I know," I replied.

My head was spinning frantically with questions. What would Erik say? How would my parents react? How could I tell them? How would I graduate? How could I ride CJ? Oh no, Lord, this couldn't be happening to me! Not right now! I felt a tear trickle down my cheek, as I grew overwhelmed with emotion.

"No, don't cry," said Alyssia. She ran over to me, and hugged me tightly.

"It will be okay," she encouraged.

"I don't know how," I sobbed. I rested my head on her shoulder, until I finally calmed myself.

"I have to tell Erik," I said.

Alyssia nodded her head. "Yes, you do."

A few minutes later, I called Erik.

"Hello?"

"Hey, we need to talk about something."

"Oh, what is it?"

"Can I come see you right now?"

"Yeah, sure."

I stashed the pregnancy test under the front seat of my car and made the trip back to Olive Branch, Mississippi. An hour later, I was pulling up into Erik's driveway, when

Majoring in Motherhood

he came outside. He looked at the worried expression on my face.

"What's wrong?" he asked.

"Get in. Let's go for a drive," I replied. Erik got in on the passenger's side, and we drove around the block.

"So, what's up?" asked Erik. He had a puzzled expression on his face.

"Well..." I paused. I couldn't bring myself to tell him.

"Just tell me," he said.

"We are in so much trouble," I replied. Erik raised his eye brows, and looked at me.

"Why?"

"I'm pregnant." The words almost seemed to hang in the air during the next few seconds of dead silence. Then, a smile came across Erik's face.

"You're pregnant?" he asked.

"Yes." I pulled the pregnancy test out from under my seat, and handed it to Erik. He stared down at it for a few minutes, before he spoke.

"Wow, okay, so what do we do now?" he asked. His voice was strangely upbeat and happy. Why wasn't he freaking out like I had predicted? What the heck was going on?

"Are you not worried?" I asked.

"Not really."

"Oh." I was utterly confused at how well Erik was

Majoring in Motherhood

taking this. He didn't seem fazed by it at all, actually. He handed me the pregnancy test, and I put it back underneath my seat. We didn't want anyone else to see it.

A few minutes later, I dropped him off at home, and headed back to college. The fifty mile drive seemed to take hours, as my head swarmed with thoughts and emotions. How was I going to take care of a baby? I didn't know anything about babies, or about being pregnant. As I pulled up at the dorms, I realized that my whole life was about to change. There was going to be no more staying out late at college parties, no more alcohol or cigarettes, no more junk food diets, no more sleeping in late, and worst of all, no more rodeos, or riding CJ. What had I gotten myself into?!

Over the next weekend, I went home to spend time with my family. It was hard to keep eye contact with them, and I was afraid that if I ate anything in front of them, they would automatically know that I was pregnant. I spent my time confused and in a daze, without knowing what to do. My parents sensed something was wrong with me, and accused me of being on drugs.

"What?! I'm not on drugs!" I yelled.

"Then why are you acting so strange?" yelled Mom.

"I'm not!"

"Yes, you are. You won't even look at us. You're guilty about something," she said.

As she stood in the kitchen, and continued to question

Majoring in Motherhood

me, Dad walked outside to search my car for evidence. "*Oh shit*," I thought. This wasn't going to end well. Surprisingly, Dad walked back inside a few minutes later without speaking a word, and sat down in the other room. After Mom had finished her rant, I ran outside to my car to make sure the pregnancy test was still under the front seat. "*Phew*," I thought. It was right where I left it.

For the rest of the day, I hung out with Erik, and we talked about what we were going to do about the situation. There was so much to think about. How were we going to afford diapers and formula? How were we going to take care of the baby? Where would we live? How would we tell our parents? Though, I would never have to tell my parents. When my father had decided to search my car for evidence, he had seen the pregnancy test, and I was just about to find that out.

My father distanced himself from me for days, and my mother blindsided me with the subject one morning. I was eating a scrambled egg, when I looked up, and realized that my mother was staring right at me.

"What?" I asked.

"Don't play dumb," she replied sternly. I swallowed down the mouthful of egg, and held my breath. Maybe I could play this one off?

"What are you talking about?" I asked.

"We know," Mom snapped.

Majoring in Motherhood

"Know what?"

"Barbra, stop being an idiot! Your father saw it!" she yelled. I pushed my plate away from me, and fought back tears.

"I'm sorry," I sobbed.

"You've really done it this time!"

"I know, I'm sorry."

There was nothing I could say that would make this situation any easier. I had dug myself a hole. My parents were furious, and upset beyond words, especially my mother. She was a strong Christian woman, who believed in abstinence until marriage, and I had failed her miserably.

That afternoon, my mother accompanied me to an obstetrician just to hear from a doctor that I was, in fact, pregnant. I was very early into the pregnancy, but having some abdominal pains, so the doctor ordered numerous blood tests and ultrasounds to make sure that the baby was developing properly. My doctor was concerned that it could be a chemical pregnancy, which is a pregnancy that develops in your fallopian tubes, and not your uterus; however, it was definitely not. I appeared to be four weeks pregnant on the ultrasound, and that sealed the deal that this baby wasn't going anywhere anytime soon.

My parents immediately began their debate about adopting the baby out, but I couldn't listen to it. If I ever had any other children, I would feel so guilty for not

Majoring in Motherhood

keeping this little baby. It was strange that I was already starting to become attached to the four week old embryo growing inside my belly. I guess that were the extreme pregnancy hormones beginning to kick in.

When Erik told his mother about my pregnancy, she was livid. Seeking out attention, she sobbed to all of her customers about my pregnancy, and how she was "too young to be a grandma." Within days, everyone around town knew I was pregnant, and asked me if it was true. Thanks a lot, Lisa.

No one was supportive of my pregnancy, or offered encouragement, but I guess that's to be expected of a teen pregnancy. If I had been my parents, I wouldn't have been too chipper about my daughter being pregnant, either. My grandparents were the only true support system I had, besides for a few "come and go" friends that enjoyed the drama of it. I would call my grandma all the time with my troubles, and she always had a way of making me feel much better.

My grandma, Barbara, was a beautiful woman. I had been named after her when I was born (and also after the nurse who saved my life), with the only difference of one letter. Even being the age that my grandma was, men around town still flirted with her, and I was not too oblivious to notice this. She had a firecracker personality, like my mother, which made her stand out in an everyday

Majoring in Motherhood

crowd.

My papaw, John, was one of the best men that I knew. He was a "handyman" to the bone, and could repair anything from plumbing problems to electrical problems, and even structural problems with buildings. Papaw never failed to have a dark tan from working in the sun so much, and a grizzly mustache. Since the day I was born, I have never remembered him looking any other way. He was just as handsome as my grandma was beautiful, and that made them the perfect couple.

When they heard of my pregnancy, they knew I would be in severe financial trouble, so they called me one afternoon with an outstanding proposition. I was currently working at a fried chicken restaurant, bringing in very little income, and my grandparents agreed to double whatever money I sent them out of my paychecks until the baby came. They knew that my tiny paychecks wouldn't go very far and they wanted to help me out during the first few critical months of the baby's life. I was thrilled! I sent them as much money out of my paychecks as I could, and my grandparents never failed to keep their word. They were such a big influence on my life and really helped me out in my time of need.

As my pregnancy progressed, so did all the unappealing symptoms. Mornings were terrible. I would wake up for school sick to my stomach and nauseous. Sometimes, so

Majoring in Motherhood

nauseous that I couldn't even bring myself to eat anything, but my mother always made me for the sake of the baby. Even though she was beyond furious, she wanted me to take good care of the innocent baby growing inside me.

    I grew moody and tired all the time, and always clung onto Erik for support that I never got. He broke my heart time and time again, and was never ashamed to throw it right in my face. It's like he enjoyed seeing me cry in front of him, like he felt empowered, or something. I didn't understand why he was always lying to me, and letting me down, but I still didn't give up on him. I needed someone to lean on, and I couldn't let go of the fact that just maybe he would go back to being the sweet Erik that I knew when we first started dating. Not to mention, that I was worried sick about raising this baby on my own without any help or support.

    Occasionally, I could feel God speaking to my heart that Erik wasn't right for me. I prayed hard that if Erik wasn't the one, that God would bless me with the Christian man who was. A man who would truly accept me and love me for who I was, despite all the mistakes I had made. However, I never really believed that God would answer my prayers. I felt like I had dug a hole that was too deep to climb out of, and that God would never fully forgive me for what I had done.

    On top of all this, my parents continued to argue with

Majoring in Motherhood

me about adopting the baby out, and how I had completely ruined my life. It was incredibly hard trying to battle against everyone about adopting my child out, but I would never stop fighting. I knew I would have to put everything on hold, including my beloved horse, but that was a sacrifice I was willing to make. I would still occasionally ride CJ, even after I had found out that I was pregnant, because I just couldn't possibly stay away from him. He was the love of my life, and I was completely heartbroken that we were becoming more and more drawn away from each other. The reality about how much this baby was going to change my life was becoming crystal clear.

One of my journal entries read,

"December 19, I really miss riding CJ all the time. That horse brings me a sense of peace that no one else can. It makes me sad to know that we won't be competing in the Germantown Charity in June. Next time, I suppose. I have dreamed of competing in this show, ever since I was twelve years old. It's divided into a hunter division and a jumper division, and on the final day, there's the Grand Prix. Oh, how I love it! I go every year to watch it, and this season would have been the one for CJ and I. I guess everything happens for a reason, though. I know CJ is sad, because I haven't been able to see him in a few weeks. I feel terrible, and this exhaustion is taking its toll on me."

Because of all the arguing, I thought long and hard about

Majoring in Motherhood

adoption. I wanted this child's life to be perfect, yet everyone was trying to convince me that this perfect life couldn't involve *me*. A baby would come with plenty of responsibilities that I was not prepared for. I was overly sarcastic, wild, and above all, immature. Those three traits were buried deep inside the person that I was, so would I be able to dig them up? I doubted myself, and jumped back and forth on the subject. My father was pro-adoption, as he could read into my sarcastic identity, but because of the rebellious person I was, whatever my father said, I was bound to do just the opposite of. I reset my mind to anti-adoption and decided I was going to keep the baby. I could do it. I know I could. I didn't have to get rid of all my traits, just a few of them. Responsibility and maturity could be added to the mix, and BAM! I would hit the jack pot. I could become the all-star mom that I needed to be, and could still be a free spirited teenager too. Right?

Majoring in Motherhood

Chapter Eight
You Were Warned

One breezy afternoon, I decided to take CJ on a ride with my dad. Mom was shocked that I would even think about riding while I was pregnant, but my stomach was still flat, and I didn't see a problem with it. I was going to eat up every opportunity I had to ride CJ, while I still could. Mom warned me that it would be a bad idea, but I ignored her, and walked up to the pasture to saddle up my horse. CJ was waiting for me at the fence line, when I got there.

"Hey old pal," I cooed. He impatiently trotted back and forth along the fence line.

"I sure have missed you!" I said excitedly. I hung the saddle on the fence, and climbed over the gate. I reached my hand out to CJ, and he pressed his velvety soft nose against my palm. It was one of my favorite things about him.

"I can see that you've missed me too," I said. He stood still as I slipped the halter over his long face, and tied him to the fence post. He watched me intently with his bright blue eyes, as I began saddling him up to ride.

"You take forever to tack up!" yelled Dad. He was already riding Nitro around the pasture.

Majoring in Motherhood

"I'm hurrying," I replied. I quickly finished saddling CJ up, and climbed aboard his broad back.

"You want to ride through the neighborhood?" asked Dad. We had gotten bored making laps around the pasture, and our neighborhood was somewhat "horse friendly."

"Totally," I replied. We made our way out of the pasture, and started riding side by side down the street.

"Come on, I'll race you!" I yelled. I kicked CJ with my heels, and he sprung into a fast gallop down the street.

"Oh no you don't!" laughed Dad. He sped Nitro up into a fast gallop, and we raced neck and neck.

"Eat my dirt!" I cried. I nudged CJ, and he sped up even faster, inching in front of Nitro.

"Yeah right," replied Dad. He pushed Nitro to the limit, and we continued to race side by side.

Suddenly, a car turned down the street, and we were forced to end the race.

"Stupid car! I totally would have won!" I trash talked.

"Keep talking," mocked Dad. We laughed, and rode the horses into a nearby field.

"I'm glad CJ is being good," said Dad.

"Yeah, me too."

I barely had time to finish the sentence, before CJ had gone from Dr. Jekyll to Mr. Hyde. He grabbed the bit between his teeth, and bolted forward without any warning.

"Whoa CJ!" I screamed, but it was no use. He threw his

Majoring in Motherhood

head between his legs, and threw his back hoofs into the air, as high as he could. He began bucking furiously, until I could barely hold on any longer.

"JUMP!" yelled Dad. I glanced down at the huge pile of rocks that was beneath me.

"I can't!" I screamed. I gripped the saddle horn as hard as I could, but nothing was going to save me. CJ arched his back so hard that it lifted me into the air, and I landed back first on the pile of sharp rocks. I felt my whole body go into shock, and I couldn't move.

"Are you alright?" asked Dad.

"I think so," I groaned. I forced myself to sit up. My back was in sheer pain, and there was blood dripping down my elbow, staining the rocks red. I turned my head and watched, as CJ sprinted toward the street.

"Get him!" I yelled. I was terrified that a car would hit him. A watching bystander ran toward the street, and stopped CJ right in his tracks. He grabbed hold of the reins, and began walking him back toward us.

"I'm sick of this horse," said Dad. He got off Nitro, and thanked the watching bystander for bringing him back to us.

After the bystander had left, Dad lost his cool with CJ. He began whipping him back and forth across the face with the reins, and screaming obscenities at him. I watched helplessly as CJ began rearing into the air, trying to avoid

Majoring in Motherhood

the leather slapping against his face.

"Stop it!" I yelled.

"Shut up!" Dad screamed. He shot me an angry glare.

I couldn't watch my father whip my horse any further, so I reached into the pocket of my jeans, and pulled out my cell phone. I called my mother, and asked her to come pick me up, since I was so distraught and could barely walk. She wasn't the least bit surprised. She arrived a few minutes later, and lectured me the whole ride home about how dangerous CJ was.

"What you did was completely foolish, Barbra," she said.

"You have to put the baby before yourself," she continued.

"Mom, I know," I replied.

"CJ could have killed you. How many times are you going to get bucked off, before you just give it up?" she asked.

"I don't know." A tear fell down the side of my face, as we pulled into our driveway. How could I give up CJ? He was the best thing I knew.

When I got inside the house, I washed all the blood from my elbow, and changed into some clean clothes. After that, Mom drove me to see my obstetrician, and she immediately ran a series of tests and ultrasounds to make sure the baby was okay.

Majoring in Motherhood

"I can't believe you rode a horse," scolded the doctor.
"I know, I'm sorry," I replied.
"Don't apologize, just don't do it again," she said.

With the help of my mother's prayers, all the tests results came back fine, and the baby wasn't harmed. That was the last time I ever really rode CJ, and I still have the scar on my elbow to remind me of it.

I wrote in my diary the next week, which read,
"January 17,
Today, I am seven weeks and four days pregnant. Only thirty two weeks and three more days left in this forty week pregnancy. Christmas totally sucked. Mom and Dad were so mad about my pregnancy that I literally got nothing. Not only that, but Dad threatened to make me move out before the baby comes, or else I have to adopt it out. Believe me, if I have to leave, I will find a way, because God gave me this baby for a reason. I mean, I can understand why they are so upset, but it still hurts. It's amazing how I am pregnant, and I have eaten less than I ever have in my entire life. Sometimes, the nausea is so bad that I want to puke at even the thought of food. I was really stupid last Saturday. I rode horses with Dad, and CJ bucked me off worse than he ever has. I hit the rocks. Everyone told me I should sell him, but I just can't. CJ and I have been through too much together. I hope all my exhaustion goes away soon, because it's getting really hard

Majoring in Motherhood

trying to juggle work and school."

As another month passed, I began to fall into a deep depression with my life. Erik and I hardly saw each other anymore, because he was always too busy with school and his "friends" and my parents just couldn't lay off the fact that I was pregnant. They said hurtful things about my pregnancy, even though there was nothing I could do to change it, and my once sarcastic and happy spirit began deteriorating. I was absolutely miserable.

As hard as school was, I still told myself that no matter what, and no matter how hard things got, I would stay in college, and get my degree for the sake of my child. I wanted to give this baby the best life I could, just like my father had given me, regardless of his hurtful comments. I could feel myself falling further away from my faith, as all the fighting, stress, and tears I cried helped to build a wall between God and I. I was angry at him for putting me through such hard times, and instead of embracing God's love, I completely denied it.

Majoring in Motherhood

<u>Chapter Nine</u>
You're Not My Hero

Over the next few months, my neighbor, Patty, began riding CJ on a daily basis. She started to fall in love with him the way I had, and I grew immensely jealous every time I saw her riding him. She and my father would go horseback riding together, while I sat in the house, and stared at the growing belly that had changed everything. I was so angry deep inside, but I knew that my life with CJ was over. I could never take care of a newborn baby and a horse, and give both of them the attention they deserved.

I hung out with Erik as much as I could, but his presence didn't help my aching heart. His reply to everything was, "maybe we should just put the baby up for adoption." I grew furious every time that those abrasive words came out of his mouth.

"This baby is just as much your responsibility as mine! I wasn't ready for a child, either, but you don't see me running away from the situation!" I yelled.

"Well, I don't think I'm ready to be a dad."

"Then, why am I pregnant, Erik?" I asked. He looked at me in the eyes for a few minutes, before he confessed the truth.

Majoring in Motherhood

"Now, you can't leave me," he said. My mind went numb.

"What did you say?"

"You can't leave me now. You're pregnant."

"Erik, what are you telling me?" I asked. My eyes were locked on him.

"I can leave you, but you can't leave me."

"Did you do this on purpose?!" I cried.

"I don't even know if that's my baby!" he yelled.

"What?!"

"My mom doesn't think it is, so we are going to have to get a DNA test."

"You stupid idiot! I hate you!" I screamed. My mind was whirling in a wild cyclone of thoughts, and I didn't know how to respond to them. What was I going to do?! This had all been a set up, and I had stupidly fallen for it!

"Get the hell out of my car!" Erik yelled.

I got out of the car, and slammed the door as hard as I could. As I stepped onto the curb of the street, he squealed his tires, and spun out of the parking lot. The cold wind sent shivers up my spine, and I realized what had just happened.

"God, why do you keep putting me through such stress?" I thought, *"Why doesn't Erik love me like he used to? What is happening to my life?!"* I sat down on the curb of the street, and cried. When I finally made it home that night, I

Majoring in Motherhood

grabbed my diary, and began writing. It read,

"I am four months pregnant now. Depression is creeping in on me fast, and nothing means much to me anymore. Stress constantly makes me want to faint. Mom and Dad are always saying hurtful things about this pregnancy, but then they say something nice. It confuses me to death. I cried on CJ's shoulder the other day, and he comforted me. That is the first time I have cried on CJ in months. He just makes me feel so calm. My boyfriend and I are far apart now, and it is though an unbreakable wall has been built between us. I no longer feel any love for him. I feel nothing. He told me he is not ready to be a father, and he never helps me with anything. He would rather be hanging out with his friends, and listening to his mom say mean things about me. He says that he loves me, but he does nothing to prove it. I just don't know what to think of anything anymore."

The next week, Erik and I started dating again, and from there on out, it was an on again-off again relationship. I don't know why I kept taking him back, but I just couldn't seem to let go. I was scared to death to be pregnant and alone, especially since I hardly had anyone to hang out with. It always seemed like when Erik's friends were busy, he came running back to me, but the minute they wanted to hang out, he was gone again. He always complained that he couldn't help me buy anything for our baby, but it was

Majoring in Motherhood

because he was too busy spending it on himself. I watched him buy movies, brand new cell phones, stuff for his car, but nothing for our baby. We fought through text messages all the time about what was important, but he always jumped back with the typical "maybe we should put the baby up for adoption." I grew to hate the lowlife that had gotten me pregnant, and I regretted having ever dated him. He would rather turn his back on his own son, than become a father. I could have never done that.

When we were hanging out, he always wanted to go eat at Huddle House. He never bought me anything to eat, and I never had any money, so I had to just sit there and watch him devour his food. After a while, I started to notice that we always had the same waitress, and Erik was always making small talk with her. Finally, I caught on. I was sick of him always hurting my feelings! He was too selfish to care about anyone, but himself! I broke up with him that night, but he wasn't daunted by losing me at all. Come to find out, he had been talking to that girl for several weeks, and when he wasn't with me, he was with her!

I cried so hard that night that I had to gasp for air. I stayed awake all night long tearing up every picture of Erik that I had and throwing away anything he had ever given me. My mother heard me crying, and came into my room to find the mess of ripped up pictures and broken objects on the floor.

Majoring in Motherhood

"When are you going to stop putting yourself through this?" she asked.

"I don't need to hear that right now! My heart is broken!" I cried.

Mom sat down next to me on the floor and comforted me, until I finally fell asleep. She was sick and tired of seeing me all worked up over someone who didn't give two cents about me, or this precious baby. I was worth more than what Erik had to offer.

A couple weeks later, Erik tried getting back together with me again, but I knew better. At the same time that he was trying to get back together with me, he was also trying to hook up with another girl from his art class, and I knew about it. I texted the girl and she confronted me with everything that Erik had been saying to her. In fact, she didn't even have a clue that I was pregnant! Once Erik found out that I had been talking with this girl, he became furious, and threatened my life. He texted me saying that I needed to die and that he wanted to kill me and the baby.

When my parents found out they were floored. They hated Erik, but they never imagined that he could say something so horrific to me. My parents became frightened that Erik might actually hurt me, so that night, my dad called the police on Erik and he was arrested shortly after. He spent only two nights in jail, but then his mom was able to bail him out. I didn't talk to Erik for weeks after that,

Majoring in Motherhood

because the police took domestic violence very seriously, and had filed a no contact order between us.

Remember how I called myself an idiot teenage girl? This right here proves it. Erik told me that he had only said those things, because he thought I had cheated on him, and asked me to go to his senior prom with him. Stupidly, I gave him the benefit of the doubt once again and believed him. Right before our court date, I went behind my parents' backs and dropped all the charges on Erik. I shouldn't have fallen for Erik's lies again, but I guess I was still holding onto whatever hope I had left that Erik would change. Again, I had made a bad decision.

The following week, Erik took me to his senior prom, and I was more than happy to go. I didn't care to think about the hurt and pain I had just been through, and going to prom with him seemed like something that I should take advantage of before the baby came. Although she was against my decision to go, my mother helped tailor a gorgeous long dress to fit my baby bump and styled my hair in beautiful waves over my shoulders. I was so excited to be going to prom with Erik; however, when we got to the restaurant to eat, he started yelling at me for putting him in jail, even though it had been beyond my control and not my fault. After that, prom night was downright horrible and I spent the first half of it in tears and the second half exhausted and miserable at the dance. Nosey people asked

Majoring in Motherhood

me about my pregnancy and if I planned to keep the baby all night long, until I couldn't stand it anymore. I just wanted to disappear off the planet.

A few weeks later, Erik joined the Navy on a whim. He decided that he wanted to serve the country and after failing the ASVAB twice, he finally took it a third time and passed by only nine points. Although he received the worst job available, he paraded around town, bragging like he was some hero. Yeah, some hero he was threatening to kill the mother of his child and his own baby. He shaved his head and started wearing military clothes to play the part, even though he hadn't even left for boot camp yet, and everyone made fun of him. I didn't understand Erik's motives, and I was beginning to see just how mentally unstable he was. He had periods of manic episodes followed by periods of depressive episodes, just like his mother. Finally, I slowly began to pull away from him.

Majoring in Motherhood

<u>Chapter Ten</u>
It's a Boy!

After being around enough toddler girls, I realized that I wanted a baby boy. I had always dreamed of having a little all-American family, and traveling around in a fancy SUV to soccer games, or maybe baseball games. I felt the baby move around and kick inside my tummy, and at first, it was such a strange feeling. Sometimes, it made me nauseous, but as time went on, I began to love the feeling of my baby move. I would pray over the little beating heart inside me every single day, that it would be the most beautiful and healthy baby.

Finally, the day of my ultrasound rolled around. It was time to see the gender of the baby. Only my mother and I went to the appointment, because Erik "couldn't go," but it was a nice bonding experience for the both of us. I was eager, as they covered my tummy in blue goo, and so was my mother. The ultrasound technician never even had to tell me what the gender of my baby was. As I watched the screen, I found out the answer for myself, and to my excitement, it was a boy! I looked over at my mother, as a tear rolled down my cheek, and she had tears rolling down her cheeks as well. These were tears of joy but also tears

Majoring in Motherhood

for fear of the future.

My diary read,

"April 8, It has been nearly a month since I have written. I attended my doctor visit on March 30, and had my ultrasound. I'm having a boy! I was so happy that I started crying, because over this last month I realized that in my heart, I wanted a boy. His name will be Noah Michael, and as of March 30, he currently weighs 11 ounces."

I fell in love with the little boy growing inside my expanding baby bump. The next day in class, I wrote this letter to him:

Dear Baby,

I can't wait to meet you. You're growing so fast. I feel you move and kick inside my tummy all the time. I love you already. I'm naming you Noah. I watched you on the ultrasound yesterday. You kicked me, rubbed your eyes, and I think you might have hiccupped. You were adorable! I convinced the ultrasound technician to give me extra photos of you. I'll save them all for you to see later. It looks like it will be just you and me, kiddo. We will bond, and I hope you will play sports. Maybe you and I can get back into a life with horses together? Eventually, you and I will set out toward the coast, so that we can live close to the ocean. You would love the beach. I love you so much.

Love,
Mommy

Majoring in Motherhood

I chose the name, Noah, for my son, as a love letter to God. In Hebrew, it means comfort from God, and somewhere else I read that it also means repentance to God. Sure, sex before marriage had been a major slip-up, but this little baby wasn't. I guess God thought I could handle having a baby, because why else would he have given me one?

A few weeks later, I got back together with Erik again to help ease the loneliness, which was again a mistake. You would think that by now I had learned my lesson. Lisa planned a baby shower for Noah, mailed out all the invitations, and then cancelled it without notifying anyone, except her close family. Her explanation was that Erik and I were fighting, and she didn't want us to be around each other. This was another one of her control tactics, and all it did was punish an innocent baby. Fine, screw your stinking baby shower! I will just get everything I need for this baby by myself. They had never even bought anything for the baby, anyway. I didn't understand the crazy woman for the life of me, but even still, I continued to show kindness to her.

A few weeks later on Lisa's birthday, Erik and I went to the store, and I bought her a beautiful gift of a glass scent diffuser and sweet smelling oils. Erik never helped me pay for any of it, as expected, but I was eager to give it to her. On the way home, Erik suddenly accused me of texting

Majoring in Motherhood

other guys, and snatched my cell phone out of my hand. He never had any trust in me, and forever accused me of hooking up with other guys, which was not true. He screamed that the baby was not his, as I pleaded otherwise.

"You whore! This baby is not even mine!"

"Erik, of course this is your baby! I have not cheated on you once!" I cried. Tears were pouring from my eyes, smearing eye liner all down my face.

"Leave me alone, don't you ever talk to me again!"

"Erik, pull over before you kill us both!" He was driving angrily between lanes, and beginning to swerve off the road.

"No! I'm not stopping! If you're scared, then get out of my car, you slut!"

I looked at him with fear. Why should I have to be risked death, just because he was obsessively convinced that I was cheating?! I prayed that God would protect the ever blameless baby that rested inside my tummy, hearing such dreadful things.

I popped his car stereo out, and held it out the window, threatening to drop it, if he didn't slow down. His face shot blood red, and he went into a rage.

"Give me my radio NOW!"

"No, not until you slow down!"

Erik took his eyes off the road, and grabbed my arm as hard as he could. I could feel my bones beginning to bend

Majoring in Motherhood

painfully, as he squeezed harder and harder.

"You're hurting me!"

"Then give me my stereo!

He gripped my other arm, and snatched the car stereo from my fingers. I was helpless, and Erik knew it, taking full advantage of the situation.

Once we finally reached his house, Erik grabbed his mother's gift out of the back seat, and slammed his door as hard as he could. His mother, who was sitting on the front porch, ran out to see what was wrong. He then filled her head with such a lie, and threw her birthday present at her, shattering it to pieces all over the driveway. I got out of the car, and approached Erik and Lisa.

"Give me my phone, I'm going home," I demanded.

"Hell no! I gave you this phone! It's mine, not yours!"

"Erik, you gave me that phone months ago, because you got a new one!"

"Well, I'm taking it back!" he screamed.

"Erik, give it to me! I'm leaving!"

He held up the phone, so that I could plainly see it, and then pitched it like a baseball toward the street as hard as he could. Seeing that not enough damage was done to it, he stomped on the phone, until nothing but broken pieces were left. Then, he proceeded to take out the SIM card, and bend it in half.

His mother, eating up the situation, just sat back and

Majoring in Motherhood

watched. By the wicked stare in her eyes, I knew she was wishing that it was me he was stomping upon. To her, I was nothing more than dirt underneath her feet that could easily be swept under a rug.

In my mind, she transformed into a hideous witch with oozing boils, and a disfigured facial structure. I was able to see right through her blemished, translucent skin, and right into the soul that was hiding behind her body. She was a malicious witch.

Erik soaked up his opportunity to belittle me, and yelled obscenities at me. He stormed over to me, grabbed my shoulders with such force, and began pushing me down the street, until I had fallen.

He screeched, "Never come back! I hate you, and I hate that baby!"

Lisa, realizing he was physically harming me, yelled at Erik to release me. Erik obeyed, and shoved me down one final time, as he released his grip. He took off running down the street, as his mother walked over to me.

"Barbra, please don't call the police on Erik again."

I just looked at her with disgust. She had not once offered to stop the rampage, which had just taken place.

"He just hurt me, Lisa," I mumbled.

"Yes, Barbra, but it takes two to fight. I'm sure you did something to set him off."

At that moment, I felt like my heart exploded. I did

Majoring in Motherhood

something? Did she really just say that when all I was doing was trying to get through this horrific pregnancy?! I'm helpless right now! How could *I* do something?!

"Lisa, I need a cell phone. He broke mine, and he owes me a new one right now. I have no way to get in touch with anyone."

"Barbra, I'm not dealing with that right now. I have enough on my plate tonight. Wasn't that Erik's phone, anyway?"

"He gave it to me!" I cried.

"Well, technically, it was still his," she insisted. I glared at her with such hate. I hoped she suffered a miserable life.

Lisa pleaded with me further not to call the police, as I sulked in sadness. I blocked out her babbling, and it became a white noise buzzing in my ear.

When I was finally able to make it home, I went to look at myself in the mirror. I had red marks and fingerprints all over my arms and shoulders from where Erik had hurt me. My parents had been out of town for the entire thing, so I called them crying hysterically. They were outraged at Erik's behavior, and furious with Lisa for not stopping it.

"Barbra, you should call the police," my father said. He was right. I definitely should have, but I didn't.

My parents were fuming with anger, and warned me not to put Erik on Noah's birth certificate. His family deserved to have nothing to do with the innocent baby. However, I

Majoring in Motherhood

knew that would never be the case, for Lisa was too committed on her attempt to destroy what little life I had left. Erik had plainly confessed that he didn't want anything to do with our baby, but Lisa wasn't going to let it go that easily. If she felt that she had any sense of control over the situation, then she was going to fight me until the end.

Chapter Eleven
It's Almost Over

Over the following weeks, I felt myself sink deeper into a depression. I was trying to run away as fast as I could, but an invisible wall stood between me and my escape. I was desperate. I longed to ride CJ more than anything in the world, but my expanding belly prohibited such fantasy. He looked so beautiful every time I glanced up at the pasture, and saw his glimmering body shining against the sun light. He looked as white as one of those fluffy bunnies you see in pet shops. When I was all alone, I would close my eyes, and envision myself running away on CJ.

Finally, my first semester of college was over, and surprisingly, I passed with good grades. I was quite content with myself for finishing school, despite all the chaos that had happened during those difficult few months. Sadly, I had to give up my next semester of college, because my due date collided with the class schedule. Likewise, my mother had also convinced me that my son deserved all the love and attention that he could get during the first few months of life. So, school would just have to wait.

During my parents' wedding anniversary week, they planned a trip to the beach, and agreed to take me with

Majoring in Motherhood

them, since I had gotten good grades. It would be the last vacation that I would ever have alone, and they wanted me to enjoy every minute of it. Strangely, Erik's family planned a vacation to the exact same place and over the exact same dates, and if that wasn't bizarre enough, Erik's parents and my parents had the exact same wedding anniversary. I was stunned!

My parents weren't exactly happy when I told them, because they were hoping to get me away from Erik for a week, but they didn't stop me from seeing him over vacation. In fact, they were completely inviting to Erik. It was Lisa that became a road block in our vacation. She refused to let me see Erik at all, because she complained it would be the last vacation she could spend with her "baby," before he left for the Navy and became a dad.

I was so upset that I started cussing Erik out over the phone. Why couldn't he just stand up against his mother, and give me the support I so desperately needed? Why didn't he love me enough to defend me? I cried and pleaded on the phone with him, but he ended up getting angry at me, and hanging up. I called him back, but he didn't answer, so I left him a voice mail that said I was breaking up with him. I couldn't keep putting myself through this stress!

Erik texted me back a few minutes later, but it wasn't the response I was hoping for. He had been talking to another

Majoring in Motherhood

girl over the last few weeks, and she had just agreed to dating him. I stared at the text message, until my eyes had filled with tears. How could he do this to me? I looked down at my pregnant belly, and closed my eyes. This was going to get a lot harder, before it got any better.

I did my best to enjoy every minute of the vacation, but it was hard trying to forget about the pain I was feeling in my heart. I was pregnant with the child of an idiot and someone who would forever put themselves above the needs of others. Why hadn't I enlisted my trust in God when he had first starting sending me subtle messages that Erik was not the right man for me? Why had I let it get this far? I sat out by the shoreline, and let the sound of the crashing waves take me away. All I wanted was to hear that someone loved me.

Finally, on the last day of vacation, Erik called and asked to see me. He apologized for what had happened earlier that week, and said his mother would allow us to see each other, but only if we complied to her rules. We could only spend half the day with my family, then we had to spend the rest of the day with his family. I was embedded with bone deep hostility toward Lisa, and I was not sure how much longer I could handle her absurd self-declared laws, but I reluctantly agreed. I know that I shouldn't have kept bringing Erik back into my life, but I toyed with the fantasy that maybe we could be a real family once the baby

Majoring in Motherhood

came and just maybe he would change. We spent the last day of vacation walking up and down the beach and trying to look past our differences, but sadly, Erik and I would never see eye to eye, and our moments together left me feeling emptier than I had before.

With all the confusion and emptiness inside my heart and mind, I began having horrible nightmares that Lisa was going to try and take Noah away from me by using Erik's name. My pregnancy hormones caused the dreams to be so surreal that I would fight wildly in my sleep night after night, until one night, I finally screamed out, "You stupid bitch!" I screamed so loud that it woke me up, as well as almost everyone else in the house. My mom came running into my room, and asked who I was screaming at, but I just sat up in my bed tiredly.

"What?" I moaned.

"Who are you screaming at?" she asked again.

"I screamed?"

"Yes, you screamed. I nearly killed myself jumping out of bed so quickly," she said. Mom put her hands on her hips, and looked at me crossly.

"I'm sorry, I must have yelled out in my sleep," I smiled. The thought of my mother rushing out of bed, and tripping all over the place was hilarious to me for some reason. Mom smiled too, and began walking back to her room. As she began to leave, she turned around and said,

Majoring in Motherhood

"Sleep well for the both of us, because I sure won't be able to fall back asleep after that."

The cool spring soon turned into the hot summer, and I was heavy with baby. I spent most of my time hanging out with Darby and Katie, since Erik was hardly ever around. Darby was also pregnant, and by the same guy she ditched me for at the football games, but her baby was due a little over a month before mine. We took a tour of the hospital where we were going to have our babies, and it suddenly hit me that I only had a month and a half left, until Noah was here. I was excited and terrified all at the same time.

A couple weeks later, I was hanging out at Darby's house, and she convinced me to help her go into labor. It was the week of her due date, and she was so tired of being pregnant, yet nothing she did seemed to work. We got on the internet and tried everything we could, until her last hope was to drink castor oil. I remember how disgusting it smelled, and how badly Darby gagged when she drank it. After that, she spent nearly the entire night in the bathroom. I felt sorry for her, but I couldn't help but laugh about it. It was hilarious how she would come out of the bathroom, talk to me for a few minutes, then grab her butt, and run back into the bathroom. Apparently, it worked, because she texted me later that night, and said that she was in the hospital having contractions. Since it was the week of her due date, the hospital kept her, and further induced her

Majoring in Motherhood

labor with Pitocin.

I got to the hospital around twelve that afternoon, and stayed there all day long, until she finally gave birth to her daughter late that evening. I got all teary eyed, as I held my best friend's baby for the first time. Within a few weeks, I would be holding *my own* son. I left the emotional entry in my diary that read,

"I have so much headed my way, and no time to prepare for it. Sometimes I don't know how to handle all the emotions and feelings I endure, but I continue on. It's exciting and terrifying at the same time that in August, I will no longer be alone. I will be a mother to a beautiful baby boy, which I will have to love and support forever. I know how bad my horse misses me too. Every time I walk out to the pasture to see him, he loves on me, and acts like it's been years since I've seen him. I miss riding him more than anything. That was the one thing that saved me from life- just taking off on my horse, and forgetting everything we left behind us. It's been way too long. The minute Noah is born, I'm going to walk out of the hospital, and go ride my horse. Then, I'll come back and the reality check will hit me. Oh, who am I kidding? I'll be a mother, a daughter, a sister, a rider, and a friend, and I'll have to walk the long road ahead. It will be scary, exciting, happy, and sad, but most of all, it will be some of the best and worst times of my life, and will leave me with memories I will have forever."

Chapter Twelve
The Best Birthday Ever

The next day, it was the fourth of July, and Erik had promised to take me to see the fireworks. I was so excited to see him, because we had finally been getting along for the last few weeks, and I needed to get out of the house for a while. Since Darby had her own baby to take care of now, there wasn't much time to hang out anymore, so I spent most of my days at home, writing in my journals. I waited and waited all day to hear from Erik, but he never called. Finally, I called him.

"Hey, are you still taking me to see the fireworks?" I asked.

"Probably not. I don't really want to go," he replied. I felt my heart sink. Of course, things never went the way they should.

"Why? I've been excited about it all day!"

"Well, I'm with my friends having a barbeque."

"But Erik, you promised me!"

"You can come over here, if you want," he offered.

"Okay," I sighed.

When I got to his friend's house, I felt completely self-conscious about my body. There were girls hanging out by

Majoring in Motherhood

the pool in their bikinis, and Erik was right up in the middle of them. I tried to hold back my anger, as I approached them.

"Hey Erik," I said. He looked up at me, and smiled.

"Hi," he replied. He stood up, and put his hands on my belly.

"This is my baby," he said to the girls.

They looked at my belly, and gave me the typical snooty sneer. I gritted my teeth, and walked past them without saying a word. I didn't want to be here. I just wanted Erik to keep his word for once, and spend some time with me.

As it started getting closer to dark, I begged and begged Erik to take me to see the fireworks. He complained that he didn't want to leave, but finally, after an hour of asking over and over again, he finally agreed. When we got to the park, we found a good place to watch, and sat down beside each other.

"Thank you for taking me. It really means a lot," I said happily.

"I'm glad I came too," he smiled.

He put his arm around me, and pulled me close to him. It was the times like this that I kept holding on to. As the fireworks started, the explosions were so loud that I think it startled Noah. I could feel him kicking and moving around, and it was weird how I could see the imprints of his foot or hand, if he pressed against my belly. I felt so calm, as I sat

Majoring in Motherhood

with Erik on the grass, and watched the fireworks sparkling in the sky. For once, I finally felt peaceful.

After the fireworks were over, we made our way back to Erik's car. His mother had recently bought him a new one, since he had graduated high school, and I hated it. It was a bright red Dodge Stratus with a loud muffler that vibrated through the whole car. The faster Erik drove, the more nauseous I felt, because I could feel the vibrations pulsing through my belly. It made me want to throw up.

"Can we just spend the night hanging out together?" I asked.

"I want to go back to my friend's house," Erik replied.

"But we never spend time together anymore," I said softly. I wanted nothing more than just a quiet night with him. I was already beginning to feel tired and worn out.

"Well, I'm going back to my friend's house."

"Erik, please."

"No."

I felt a tear trickle down my face. Why did things have to be this way? Why didn't my feelings matter? My heart was so hungry for a love that Erik just couldn't give. Surely, there had to be someone else out there for me. Love wasn't supposed to be this way!

As we pulled onto the street, Erik began yelling and cussing furiously at the amount of backed up traffic.

"Calm down. It's no big deal," I said.

Majoring in Motherhood

"No! This pisses me off! This is why I didn't want to come!" he screamed.

"Why? It's just traffic. Please stop being so angry all the time," I said cautiously.

"Just shut up," Erik replied. I looked up at him with tears in my eyes. I was sick of being treated like a worthless rag doll.

"No, I won't shut up! I'm sick of you treating me this way!" I yelled.

"Then get out of my car you nasty slut!"

"I'm not a slut! I've done nothing wrong!"

Erik reached over my belly, and grabbed the door handle, yanking the car door open. Then, he started pushing me out the door as hard as he could.

"Erik, what are you doing?!" I cried.

"Get out of my car!" he screamed.

"No, you're driving! I'll die!"

I grabbed the car door and yanked it shut, as Erik pulled onto the highway. He floored the gas, until his car couldn't drive any faster, and we began swerving all over the road.

"Take me home! I want to go home!" I cried.

"NO!" screamed Erik.

I watched as we drove straight past my house, and continued down the highway. Tears poured out of my eyes, and my heart was pounding at a million miles an hour. What was he going to do to me?! I hoped that a cop was

Majoring in Motherhood

hidden off the side of the road somewhere, waiting for speeders, but there wasn't one. I closed my eyes, and began praying to God as hard as I could. If anyone could save us, it was him.

A few minutes later, Erik parked his car in a deserted gas station. My face was red and blotchy from crying so hard, and I had a pounding headache. I had never been filled with so much fear in my life. I kept silent, as Erik got out of the car, and slammed the door shut. He walked to the front of his car, sat down on the hood, and began crying hysterically. I ignored him for the longest time, until I finally gathered enough nerves to approach him.

"What is wrong with you?" I asked.

"I don't know," he cried. He buried his face in his hands, and trembled.

"Let's go home," I whispered.

Erik lifted his head from his hands, and stared at me. Then, he reached out his hand. I stared at him cautiously for a few seconds, before I took his trembling hand. He pulled me close to him, and hugged me tightly.

"I'm sorry," he said quietly.

"It's okay," I whispered. I didn't understand why I had such a compassionate nature toward Erik, but I just did. No matter how badly he scared me or hurt my feelings, I always felt that I could help him in some way, and I continued to pray for him.

Majoring in Motherhood

I was nervous as I got back inside Erik's car, but he safely drove me home without speeding. I told him good night, and made sure I didn't look like I had been crying, before I entered my house. I didn't want my parents to know what had just happened, because they would have made it really hard on me to see him again. I knew in my heart that I needed to break free of him, but I was afraid to. Without Erik, I would have had no one. And now that I look back on it, having no one would have been the smarter decision.

Two weeks later, it was my birthday, and it was by far the *worst* birthday I have ever had in my entire life. I started having painful contractions and bleeding, so I contacted my doctor right away. She sent me to the emergency room where they hooked me up on an IV and monitors. I was hoping I would go into labor early and have Noah on my birthday, but instead, I had a terrible kidney infection that was causing bad side effects on my body. To make things worse, when the nurse left the room, I lost all feeling in my body, and I went completely numb. It felt like I had passed out, while I was wide awake. It sent me into a panic attack, and my doctor made me stay at the hospital for several days.

I spent over three days in the hospital with my mother, and she never once left my side. It made me really appreciate the company I had from my mom, because I

Majoring in Motherhood

didn't have anyone else. Darby came to see me for a few minutes, but she couldn't stay long, since she had a newborn with her, and Erik refused to come see me. He texted me, saying awfully mean things, and denied that the baby was his. I didn't understand why Erik would say hurtful things to me, and especially on my birthday, but I was too use to these things to even cry. I was about to be a mother to an innocent child who needed my support more than anyone, and I wasn't going to let anything interfere with that. I had a burning sensation in my heart that if I didn't let go of Erik, my life was going to whirlwind into disaster, and finally, I was ready to listen to that feeling. I felt like I had been backed into a corner with no way out, and I decided that I would give God a chance. Nothing in my life seemed to go right, so maybe God could help heal me from the hurt of my mistakes? I needed peace so badly, and at this point, I was willing to give *anything* a shot. My mother sat silently with me, as I closed my eyes to pray that night in the hospital. It was on that day that I looked to God for help, and he had been waiting on me the whole time.

Majoring in Motherhood

Chapter Thirteen
Is it Tomorrow Yet?

It seemed like weeks upon weeks before the month of my due date rolled around, but finally, my last month of pregnancy was here. It was August. Every morning, I awoke wondering if it would be the day that I would finally meet my son, but it seemed like that day was never going to come. I was beginning to have contractions at night, but it was just false labor pains. The grand finale was yet to come.

As my pregnancy came to a close, my father listed CJ on the internet to try and sell him, before the baby came. I was heartbroken, but there wasn't a thing I could do to stop it other than pray God's will over the situation. Only He knew how much I loved my horse. Within a few days, there were some interested people on their way to see CJ. It wasn't often that you came across a solid white Quarter Horse, and especially one that was registered with a champion pedigree. I cringed at the thought of someone else taking home my horse, because he was my best friend. I had spent years with him.

When the people arrived, they couldn't help but stare at

Majoring in Motherhood

my pregnant belly, because it was huge. They were shocked to find out that I had been the one who had stood out in the summer heat, grooming CJ top to bottom, picking out his hooves, and bathing him. That horse was shining like a new penny, and he looked beautiful!

Our neighbor, Patty, tacked him up, and climbed up into the saddle. She had been the one who was riding him, since my pregnancy, and she was just as sad as I was to see him go. I caught a glimpse of a tear in her eye, as she trotted CJ around the pasture. She walked him, trotted him, and galloped, as the buyers took note of how well CJ was behaved. He obeyed Patty's every command, and was quick to change lead. The buyers asked Patty to take him around some barrels, and that's when everything changed.

CJ high tailed it around the first barrel determinedly, and galloped toward the second barrel. As CJ came around the second barrel, he suddenly had a wild look in his eye, and reared straight into the air.

"Oh my gosh!" I screamed.

"Hold on, Patty!" yelled Mom.

CJ began bucking furiously, and threw his head back so hard that he knocked Patty out. She went limp in the saddle, as CJ swung her around in every different direction. I watched as CJ leapt straight off the ground with his back arched so high, that he sent Patty flying ten feet into the air. She hit the ground with a loud thud, and everyone went

Majoring in Motherhood

running to make sure she was okay. I watched my father grab CJ by the reins, and begin beating him violently. Needless to say, the buyers left in a jiffy.

As we helped Patty off the ground, she began mumbling subconsciously, and saying that she was perfectly fine; however, she was not. Her arm was swelling up rapidly, and she had a terrible black eye. Mom helped her over to the four wheeler, and we drove her home quickly. Her husband was not too happy when he saw the condition his wife was in.

"I told you not to ride that horse," he scoffed.

"I'm so sorry Mr. Walters," I said, "I'm sorry CJ acted like he did." I felt terrible for what my horse had done to Patty, but there was nothing I could have done to stop it. I hadn't ridden CJ in months, and he had always had this wild side to him.

The next day, we found out that CJ had fractured Patty's arm. That was the breaking point for my father, and CJ was to be sold immediately. He planned to take him to the very next horse auction, and there was nothing I could say to change things. CJ's actions had only gotten worse over the last few months, and my family was sick of putting up with him. All they saw him as was a walking lawsuit. I knew in my heart that all CJ needed was a good trainer, but there was nothing that would change my parents' minds. They were scared to death that I would ride CJ again after

Majoring in Motherhood

the birth of my son, and CJ would kill me.

I spent night after night crying alone in my room. I was completely distraught that I would never ride CJ again in my life. He had been my saving grace and escape for so long, and now, I would never experience the thrill of riding him ever again. To make matters worse, Erik was hanging out with yet another girl, and lying straight to my face about it. I saw it as cheating, whether they were "just hanging out," or not. He didn't care that I needed him more than ever, because he was always too busy trying to please himself. Erik's family was also still trying to pressure me into adopting the baby out, because they didn't want it to ruin his life. They gave me numerous business cards with the names of adoption agencies on them, but I always ripped them up right in front of their faces. I didn't care how hatefully they talked about this baby, or how hard they tried to act like nothing ever happened, because this sweet baby wasn't theirs. This was *my* baby, and I was going to love and protect him like a mother should. I spent every night praying as hard as I could to God, and asking him to change my life. I asked him to bring a man into my life who would never leave, and one that would become a father to this innocent child. It was obvious to me that Erik would never be able to put aside his own desires to help fill the needs of a son, and surely that was not God's will for this baby.

Majoring in Motherhood

After being in and out of the hospital numerous times for "false labor," my doctor arranged for me to be induced the very next day. I prayed hard that night and pleaded with God to please bless the baby that was going to be born, despite the careless person I had been. I felt so sorry for the baby that was being born into this crazy mess of a life I had, but I promised to love him forever no matter what. It was a wonderful and scary feeling to know that this dreadful pregnancy was finally almost over. That night, I left an entry in my diary that read,

Dear Diary,

Tomorrow, my life will change forever. Tomorrow I am getting induced at five o'clock in the evening. All the waiting, dreaming, preparing, and anticipation will be over. Noah is coming! I will be exactly thirty nine weeks pregnant tomorrow, so Noah is fully baked and ready to go. I am so excited that I could jump up and down! Finally, after all these difficult months, I will meet my son! It's such a bittersweet feeling to know that at nineteen years old, I am a mother. I am now fully responsible for another human being. Noah, I love you, and I can't wait to meet you!

Love, Mommy

Majoring in Motherhood

<u>Chapter Fourteen</u>
Delivery Room Drama

Dear Diary,
Today is the day! It's show time. It's about 3:00 and I have to leave for the hospital in about an hour. My room is spotless and everything is in perfect order for Noah. I can't believe Noah is making his big appearance soon! I pray this labor goes smoothly, and there are no complications."

I was ready to have this baby; however, I couldn't deny the fact that my heart was about to beat out of my chest. The drive to the hospital seemed to take forever. When I finally got there, they strapped cords around me to listen to the baby's heartbeat, and to record my contractions. Then, they hooked me up to an IV, and started me on fluids. I was able to sleep through the night, but at 5 o'clock in the morning, they started running Pitocin in my IV. It only took about an hour to kick in, before I really started to feel the pain. The contractions pulsed through my entire body, like the worst yellow jacket sting you could ever imagine. It was too painful to even move, and every time another contraction shot through my body, I would become motionless and silent. I didn't want anyone to talk to me, or touch me. The contractions were rapidly elevating on

Majoring in Motherhood

the monitor, and I was dreading every single one.

Surprisingly, Erik actually showed up, but it would have been better had he not. His family kept barging their way into my delivery room, and harassing me, while I was in terrible pain. There was a sign on my door that read, "*No visitors*," but they refused to take orders from anyone, even the nurses. My labor was intensely stressful, as Erik's family jealously tried to prove that they had rights to be in the room with me.

Right after I had received my epidural, Erik's aunt shoved past my poor grandmother, and waltzed right into my delivery room. We had never been close, and she had always stuck her nose up at me anytime I had been at one of Erik's family occasions, so I knew for a fact that she wasn't there to be supportive for me. She was a sorry excuse for a woman, having cheated on her husband, and divorcing him for an older guy with more money. She was on the heavier side of the scale with noticeably dyed blonde hair that was chopped off above her shoulders, which made her round face, even rounder.

"Barbra," she started, "how are you feeling? Everyone in the waiting room wants to know, so I told them I would come find out."

"You need to leave," said my grandmother. "The note on the door says to check with the nurses first, because she doesn't want any visitors."

Majoring in Motherhood

   Erik's aunt deliberately ignored my grandmother, and continued on.
   "So, you just got your epidural? I bet you're loopy. When I got my epidural years ago, I felt like the wallpaper on the walls were talking to me."
   "Oh," I mumbled. I wanted to kick the woman in the face. She was such an idiot! Why didn't she just leave me alone? She was making herself out to be a fool, and I was in no condition to be having a conversation with anyone. I mumbled something else, I don't even remember what, and then rolled over. All I wanted was peace and quiet. I don't even remember Erik's aunt leaving my delivery room.
   My epidural messed up three times, sending me into a panic. An alarm would go off, and the nurses would run into my room, and scare the hell out of me. I remember one of them saying, "Oh no, it's in the wrong place in her spine!" Sometimes, I thought they were panicking just as bad as I was.
   At last, it was show time. I was fully dilated and fully effaced. I pushed for over an hour while Erik's biological dad and his girlfriend continually tried to work their way into my room. They were both employees at the hospital from other wings, and they furiously tried to use their hospital badges to bust into my room, while I was delivering my son. It was awful. They yelled obscenities at my mother and grandmother for not allowing them into

Majoring in Motherhood

the room, causing my delivery to be so much more stressful than it needed to be. I was about to explode with anger. Erik's dad's girlfriend even put her hands on my mother and shoved her, because my mom was trying to keep the door to my room closed! When the doctor saw that, she screamed for the nurses to guard my door immediately, and to keep everyone out. Erik's dad was forced to leave, but not before he yelled at my mother, and called her a bitch. I should have had him and his girlfriend fired from the hospital, because I had plenty of witnesses, but for whatever the reason, I didn't.

It was the most excruciating twenty six hours of pain I will ever remember, and I will never forget how tiring and stressful it was. The birth of my son could not have come soon enough. Finally, at 6:09 in the evening, my son, Noah Michael, was born. I was flat out *exhausted*. I don't even remember holding my son for the first time, because I was so tired. The only thing I remember is throwing up, once everyone had come into my delivery room, and that is it. I bet I sure looked good after delivery! One of my friends even told me that there was still blood on the floor. Wow.

When I was recovered enough, I was more than anxious to truly take a look at my Noah. I thought he was the most beautiful baby that I had ever laid eyes on, and he was all mine. He reminded me of a fragile porcelain doll with his smooth skin and gentle face. He had a thick, beautiful head

Majoring in Motherhood

of bright red hair and big blue baby eyes. I was in love instantly. He weighed seven pounds, fourteen ounces, and twenty one inches long. Not bad for a girl of my size.

At just fifteen hours old, Noah was so alert; making faces, looking around, and he even smiled. Everyone fell in love with the baby, even my father who had so admittedly been against the entire pregnancy. All my friends, family, and all of Erik's extended family came to the hospital to meet the infamous baby Noah. I was not too excited about seeing Erik's ever so gossipy family, but it was nice having all my friends together in one place, since that never happened. I remember Darby telling me how beautiful he was, as she sat holding him in a chair in the corner. I couldn't help but feel proud of the little baby I had given birth to. I was one happy mother.

The same night Noah was born, Erik's mother, Lisa, was so adamant on seeking attention off of her new grandson and onto herself, that she ran away from home. Her husband, Steve, called Erik to explain that they had gotten into a fight, and to ask him to help find his mother. Without any hesitation, Erik left his newly born son, and went to look for his mother. Erik had one of those families who loved to be completely soaked up in unnecessary drama, just so that they could have something to talk about the next day. I was angry that Erik would even fall for such ridiculousness, but I just kept it to myself. He just

Majoring in Motherhood

continued to keep proving to me what kind of person he truly was.

When Erik returned a few hours later, he had a long scratch all the way down his forearm. He said that once he had found his mother, they got into a fight, and he grabbed her car keys out of her hand. When he did, she scratched him, and threatened to call the police on him, if he didn't hand her the keys. Erik handed over the keys at the word "police," and watched as his mother drove off. Lisa then proceeded to spend one night in a hotel room, before returning home. Her unstable mood scared me, and I feared for my beloved new son being around her. Stupidly, I had let Erik sign the birth certificate, and from that moment on, I wished I would have listened to my parents.

Majoring in Motherhood

Chapter Fifteen
The Baby Comes First

Life with a newborn baby was more than hard, sometimes, it even felt almost impossible. I became delirious from lack of rest. The minute I would fall asleep, Noah would wake up. Sometimes, my mother would wake up, and help me in the middle of the night with Noah. She was such a great help and she was my only help. Erik never once took care of Noah, or even changed a single diaper, and it was always all on me. He would come over for a few hours, sit around while I took care of Noah, and then leave when his mother would call and tell him to come home. Yes, Lisa continued to control Erik, even though he was grown, and now had his own son to support. She was his master, and he was none other than a puppet wrapped around her feeble finger. I think that Lisa thought she could manipulate the situation however she pleased, but I was not about to stand for it any longer. Not since I had a son of my own to worry about.

My father resented Erik so much that he went into the baby's room one day, and got rid of any clothing Noah had that related him to his dad. I had a particular baby bib that had "*I Love Daddy*" written on it, and my dad grabbed the

Majoring in Motherhood

bib and put it on the dog. He then managed to find a onesie that said *"Daddy Rocks"* on it, and dressed our poor little Jack Russell terrier in the onesie and bib. The dog looked hilarious dressed in baby's clothes, and I couldn't help but bust out laughing. My father then proceeded to open the back door, and let the dog run wild for a couple hours, before letting her back inside. When my dad let her back in, the baby clothes were quite a sight to see. The bib was tattered and torn, the onesie was covered in mud and dog fur, and all of it smelled horribly of filthy rotten dog. I guess that was the only way my father could legally take out his anger on Erik, but it sure made for one funny afternoon.

    I made the decision to breast feed Noah, because I read that it strengthened their immune system to protect against sickness, and I wanted to be sure that I did everything in my power to make Noah the healthiest baby he could be. However, it turned out to be much more difficult than I had envisioned. Every time the baby was hungry, you had to be right there. You were a walking food source around the clock. Not only that, but you had to eat enough food to produce enough milk, yet I was hardly ever eating from all the stress of raising a newborn. It was also hard trying to make sure the baby was consuming enough food, since you couldn't measure what the baby was getting. I started pumping before Noah's feeding time, so that I knew exactly

Majoring in Motherhood

how much he was getting. Waking up in the middle of the night to feed Noah never got any easier, but I didn't have a choice. I guess that's just part of being a good mother.

Along with always feeding Noah, I was continually changing diapers, burping him, rocking him back to sleep, and playing with him. There was never even time to watch television, unless Noah was snuggled up beside me. I prayed peace upon the situation, and sure enough, God heard my prayer. He knew I meant it this time. He made the situation easier, and helped to ease motherhood on me. Noah consumed all my time and energy, yet he never ceased to make me smile. He was such a happy baby, and it made all the lack of sleep and energy worth it when that baby would coo at me. He would give me the gummiest smile ever, like he was the happiest baby in the world, and he would make the sweetest little sounds. Regardless of my life going haywire, I still couldn't help but fall in love with my little boy.

When Noah turned two weeks old, our family took a trip to California. Noah was excellent on the plane ride. He slept soundly in my lap the whole ride, and woke up only once to eat. I had pumped out all of his bottles beforehand, because I was not about to whip out what God had given me in front of everyone else on the plane! I always hated seeing mothers feed their babies in public, because it seemed disrespectful to everyone else around them.

Majoring in Motherhood

Once we got to California, I couldn't help but get excited. It was nice to let go of my connections to Erik and his mother for a couple weeks, and just concentrate on Noah. I actually felt like I could breathe, and it was easier not to stress out over the simplest things. Noah seemed to love the beach. I took him on a stroller ride by the water a couple of times, and he would always fall asleep with the ocean breeze surrounding him. At only two weeks old, Noah got to tour Beverly Hills, take a stroller ride on the Hollywood Walk of Fame, and go to Disneyland. It was actually a lot of fun taking my baby all over the place, because I never once got lonely, and I always had my little companion right there with me.

Before I knew it, our few weeks in California were gone, and it was time to return home. I felt sadness creep over me, as I packed my suitcase. I didn't want to return home to the reality of being harassed on a daily basis by Erik and his mother. As we arrived at the airport, black clouds began to roll over, and thunder boomed throughout the sky. Deep inside, I also felt a storm inside my heart. I couldn't seem to fight the sadness I held about returning home, and I just wanted to run away as far as I could, and never look back.

Returning home was just as bad as I had anticipated it to be. The whole time I had been in California, Lisa was spreading word through her customers about what a bad

Majoring in Motherhood

mother I was, and little did she know that it had gotten back to me. Not only that, but she was also pressuring Erik into forcing me to get a DNA test on Noah, because she wanted to know if she had any legal rights to my son. I was full of deep hate for Lisa for all the stress she was surrounding my life in, but I knew that eventually God would pull through for me. He hadn't forgotten about me, and all I had to do was just wait for him to show his mercy on me.

I became immersed in my writing during any free time that I had, and it helped me to deal with the changes my life was going through. With all the negativity that cascaded around me, I tried to keep my writing upbeat and happy. One afternoon, I left a cheery entry in my diary about our trip to California, which read,

"Hello Diary,

Noah is doing great, and I love him more than ever. He is such a good baby, and he hardly ever cries. He only cries if he needs a diaper change, is hungry, his tummy hurts, he is cold, or he wants his pacifier. He is awesome! He sleeps almost all the way through the night now, and he will normally wake up around midnight, and four o'clock in the morning to eat.

California was awesome! It was the best fun I have had in a while. Noah went to so many cool places at only two weeks old. We went to Beverly Hills, Laguna Beach, and Hollywood. We also went to Disneyland, the Hollywood

Majoring in Motherhood

Walk of Fame, and Rodeo Drive. Noah got to ride two of the Disneyland rides, and got his picture taken with the characters from Pirates of the Caribbean. He was so good on the plane ride there and back, and slept soundly in my lap the whole time. I had to switch to formula, while we were in California. It was just too stressful on me trying to breastfeed, while we were traveling all over the place. I'm proud of myself for breastfeeding for as long as I did, though. It's a lot harder than it looks!"

As I tried to keep my head up, it just seemed to get harder and harder to stay positive. Erik's grandparents invited me over for dinner one night, and I stupidly thought they were just trying to be nice to me. When I got there, Erik showed up a few minutes later, and it only turned into a huge argument about why Noah needed to be DNA tested. There was never even any dinner to be served. I grabbed Noah, and ran outside to call my parents.

"Mom, it was a trick! They just wanted to harass me about getting a DNA test on Noah!" I cried.

"Those idiots! Don't get one. Tell them no," Mom replied. Suddenly, Dad grabbed the phone.

"Barbra, just do it, so they'll leave you alone," said Dad. "We all already know it's Erik's kid."

"I know, but I feel like I'm getting forced into it," I replied. "It's none of their business at all. It's between me and Erik."

Majoring in Motherhood

"Well, unfortunately, Erik is wrapped around his family, and he's never going to change," replied Dad. "When are you going to just let go of him?"

I closed my eyes, and cleared my mind for a moment. Dad was right. When was I going to just let go?

"Get the DNA test, but tell Erik's grandparents that only you and Erik get to open the results," said Dad.

"Okay," I replied.

I got off the phone with my parents, and walked back into Erik's grandparents' house.

"I'll get the DNA test on my son," I said, "but only Erik and I can open the results."

I didn't even give them time to respond, before I had slammed the door shut. I strapped Noah into his car seat, and drove home in tears. I had dealt with so much judgment and rudeness from Erik's family over the last nine months of my pregnancy, and it was going to come to a halt. They hadn't been the ones to go through a twenty six hour labor, and they hadn't been the ones to stay awake with my son all night. This was the final straw. Erik and I were done.

Chapter Sixteen
Breaking Point

A few days later, Lisa invited me over for dinner to talk. She swore that she didn't have anything up her sleeve, and just wanted Erik and I to discuss a visitation schedule for Noah. I felt my blood boil at the thought of having to see Erik again, but I reluctantly showed up for dinner that evening.

As we sat around the table discussing who would have Noah on what day, Erik suddenly got up and walked out of the room.

"Where are you going?" I asked.

"To work on my car," he shrugged.

"We have to work this out," I replied.

"Just talk it over with my mom. I don't care," he mumbled. I sat quietly for as long as I could, until I finally lost it. I picked up Noah, and walked out to the garage where Erik was zip tying something into his motor.

"I have had it!" I screamed. "You don't care about anything in the world, unless it's about you. This is *not* your mom's son. This is *our* son, and if you're not going to sit down and talk this through with me, then you're not going to see him at all."

Majoring in Motherhood

"I don't care one bit! Just get the hell out of my house! Both of you!" Erik yelled. He started shoving me toward the street, while I was holding Noah, but I fought him off violently.

"Don't you dare put your hands on me, while I'm holding my baby! You may be able to hurt me, but I will *not* let you hurt my son!" I screamed. This was the breaking point for me and at that moment, all the love and compassion I had for Erik completely vanished. I wanted to tear his head off and stomp upon his head like he had my telephone. I wanted to rip his heart out of his chest and let him feel the pain and hurt I had suffered, because of him. I wanted to break his bones and make him feel the excruciating pain of childbirth. I had dealt with Erik's abuse to me, but I would *never* deal with Erik abusing Noah right in front of me. That proved to me right then just how worthless Erik was, and I promised Noah that his father would never lay a finger on him.

I grabbed Noah's diaper bag, and walked far enough away from Erik to where I felt safe. I sat down on the curb, and called my mother to come pick us up. She showed up quickly, and helped me get Noah into the car, while Lisa tried to explain herself. After enough of her babbling, my mother finally told Lisa that she had heard enough of her excuses, and that this was over. That was the last time I ever stepped foot inside Erik's house, and I have never

Majoring in Motherhood

looked back since.

After the results of the DNA test came back, all hell broke loose. Erik's grandparents never kept their word, and opened the results, which revealed that Erik was the father of Noah. Imagine that. After they had all the information they needed, they began trying to get rights to Noah. Erik's family would blow my phone up, asking if they could see Noah, and I would always reluctantly agree. I knew they were recording everything I said, and that they were going to try and use it against me in court, so I kept my nose clean. I offered to meet them for lunch, at the park, at the zoo, or anywhere they wanted, but I refused to go over to their house after all the stress and hate they had shown me. I didn't want to be put in a spot where I felt uncomfortable, and I wasn't going to let them push me around any longer. It was my way or the highway.

Despite always offering visitation to Erik's family, Erik himself never actually wanted to see Noah. It was always his mom or stepdad that called me, and when I would offer to meet them somewhere, they would decline it. They wanted me to bring Noah to their house, and drop him off and leave, but that was not about to happen. I didn't trust their motives or their mental stability, and I wasn't going to leave my son in a place where I didn't feel he was safe. If they didn't want to see my son while I was there, then they weren't going to see him at all.

Majoring in Motherhood

As I tried to establish custody of Noah, Lisa did everything she could to stop me from doing so. She got a lawyer in Erik's name, wrote out the entire contract herself, and had Erik sign it. For a while, I was only able to get temporary custody of Noah, and Erik got him one day a week, but it was really Lisa who got Noah. Erik would leave and go do other things with his friends, while Lisa and Steve cared for Noah at home.

Erik's mother and stepfather tried to get legal custody of Noah using Erik's name, so that they could manipulate the future I had planned out for my son. They even tried to write in our agreement that I could not move more than ninety miles away from their town, until Noah was eighteen years old, and that I had to verify everything I planned to do with Noah with them first. Lisa tried to control everything else, so why not try to control where I could live, or how I raised my son? She tried to establish grandparent rights, so that I would always have to give Noah to her by law. In other words, she tried to do everything in the book to ruin my life, but she was never able to succeed, because God was finally stepping up to the plate. I had waited patiently for my time to come, and it was here.

It seemed like I dealt with a hundred lawyer visits and court dates, but I would never stop fighting for my son. He was my blood, my life, and my heart. Every time another

Majoring in Motherhood

court date rolled around, my heart would drop into my stomach, and nervousness would overwhelm my thin body. My parents always told me that Lisa was a crazy woman, and that she was going to fight tooth and nail for Noah, just to prove that she had control. And my parents never failed to be right. Would this go on forever? Would I ever be able to break free of detestable Erik? I was worried sick that I would lose my son, but nothing would change the will that God had laid out for our lives. I looked to him for the protection of Noah, and he answered my prayers every single time.

The walls inside the court room felt like a prison. It seemed like a never ending battle. Hours would pass so slow that I felt like my body was glued to the seat, and I would never get to leave. The judge was a fat white man with stringy grey hair that was slopped onto his head. Not attractive by any means, if you ask me. I would sit several rows behind Lisa, Erik, and Steve, fuming hot with anger. So many times, I wanted to climb over the bench and strangle Lisa, until she could no longer breathe problems into my already disrupted life. I had plenty of ammo I could fire at them, if they really wanted to take this custody battle to the next level, but fear still consumed me. It was the judge's decision no matter what I said. I had refused to sign anything that allowed Lisa any court ordered visitation to Noah, as I knew she would hold me to that for the rest of

Majoring in Motherhood

my life, being the woman that she was. She cried when I wouldn't let her take Noah from me, yet she didn't care enough about him to meet me one afternoon to see him.

Every time Noah had to go to her house, I always feared something would happen to him. She never took care of Noah the way she should have, and that infuriated me, because I had poured out all my heart and soul into that little boy. He was my everything. I prayed God's will over Noah's custody, as I didn't have money to continue to fight her in court. As a new mother, I barely had any money at all. Diapers, formula, bottles, and baby clothes ate holes inside my pockets.

I prayed that God would bring peace into my life. I really needed peace. With so much confusion and worrying all the time, stress consumed my body. I could never sleep. Awake late at night, I would dream myself away to a cozy cottage surrounded by acres upon acres of unfenced, wide open pastures. A place where CJ and I could run free without the chains of our lives bound around our bodies. I continued to seek comfort from CJ, even though I barely had any time to see him.

Finally, Lisa stopped fighting for rights, and I was able to have some peace with my son. With Erik trying to go into the Navy, he could not have any custody of any dependents, not that he even deserved it. He signed Noah over to me with full custody, and the fight was over at last.

Majoring in Motherhood

God had heard all my prayers, and had shown his grace over little Noah. We had won.

Chapter Seventeen
A New Beginning

When Noah turned five weeks old, my entire life changed forever. After all the turmoil, sadness, and strife I had endured, I finally met the person that God had chosen for me to spend the rest of my life with. His name was Sam.

I was on MySpace one afternoon, while Noah was napping, and I casually came across Sam's profile. Although I had never met him, I noticed that he was excessively handsome, and a couple of our friends knew each other, so I sent him a message. It simply said, "*You're adorable.*" I never honestly believed that I would ever meet this guy, but a few hours later, I got a sweet reply from him. He said he thought I was beautiful, and had come across my profile a few days ago, but was too nervous to say anything to me. After that, I sent him my phone number, and we texted back and forth for a few hours. I asked him what his favorite band was, and when he replied with my favorite, I knew I wanted to meet him right then and there. Most people had never even heard of my favorite band, but Sam was one of the few who did. I sent him a text to call me, and within a few minutes, my

Majoring in Motherhood

phone was buzzing. I felt my heart start beating faster, as I answered the phone.

"Hello?" I asked.

"Hey," said Sam. His voice was handsome, just like I had imagined it to be.

"I want to meet you," I said.

"Now?"

"Yes, right now," I answered. It was already eight o'clock in the evening, and he lived in the next town over, but I just *had* to meet him.

"Okay, where do you want to meet?" he asked.

"What about at the movies?"

"Okay, sounds good."

We agreed to meet at the very next showing of some lame alien movie, and I called my friend, Megan, to go with me. If Sam turned out to be some crazy stalker or murderer, we could make a quick getaway together. Now, I just needed to get permission from my mother. I sat on the corner of her bed, where she was watching television, and waited for a commercial, so I could ask. Finally, a stupid commercial for tampons came on.

"Mom?" I asked cautiously.

"What is it?" she asked.

"There's this guy I would really like to go meet right now. He's very cute, and Megan is going to go with me," I said.

Majoring in Motherhood

"So, I guess you want me to watch Noah?" Mom asked. She folded her arms, and looked at me.

"If it wouldn't be too much to ask," I replied.

"Just who is this guy?" she asked.

"Oh, he's so cute! Come look at his pictures!" I said excitedly.

After Mom had inspected Sam's pictures and profile, she agreed to watch Noah for the night. I was so happy that I could have jumped up and down, but instead, I just gave my mother a huge hug, and got all Noah's things together for her. Luckily, my parents had so kindly given me their minivan, so I had a safe vehicle to drive around in. I loved that van, and I personalized it perfectly just for Noah and I. I had navy blue racing stripes painted down hood and rear of the van, and set up the inside of the van with toys and mirrors for Noah to look at. Everyone around town knew me as the girl with the "racing van," and it was the only car that Noah ever rode in. It was our "home on wheels" and we loved that old reliable van as if it were part of the family.

After Megan had arrived, I kissed my sleeping son good-bye, and we drove thirty minutes to the cinema located in the town Sam lived in.

"I'm so nervous," I whispered to Megan.

"Yeah I would be too," she smiled.

A few minutes later, I saw Sam walk around the corner.

Majoring in Motherhood

He looked almost identical to his picture, and he had a big smile on his face. He recognized me instantly.

"Hey," he smiled.

"Hello," I replied.

"And you must be the best friend," Sam said to Megan. She smiled and waved at him from behind me.

Once we walked up to the ticket counter, Sam surprised both Megan and I by buying not only my ticket, but Megan's ticket too, and also whatever snacks and drinks we wanted.

"He's really sweet," whispered Megan.

"I know," I gushed.

We sat through the most boring two hour alien movie I have ever seen, but it was still one of the best dates I have ever been on in my entire life. I ached to hold Sam's hand the entire time, and I knew he was thinking the same thing, but we were both too nervous to make that first move. When the movie finally ended, we all walked out to the parking lot, and talked for hours. We shared funny stories, sad stories, and hate stories, and all three of us quickly became close friends. The more Sam revealed himself to me, the more I fell for him. He was so genuine in a way that I can't describe, and within those first few hours of meeting, I knew in my heart that I would see him again.

Finally, at two o'clock in the morning, I got a phone call from my mother that it was time to come home. We had all

Majoring in Motherhood

been so lost in our conversation that we hadn't realized what time it was. We all agreed to meet up the very next day, because I was going to need all the emotional support I could get. My father was taking CJ to an auction, and there was nothing that I could do or say to change his mind. I was feeling sadder and more insecure than I had ever felt before, because I would have to part ways with the horse who had been through it all with me.

As we all got in our cars to leave, I quickly ran up to Sam, and kissed him on the cheek. I was too nervous to stick around for the result, so before Sam could say anything, I hightailed it back to my car. As we drove away, I caught a glimpse of Sam sitting in his car with the biggest grin on his face I'd ever seen. It was obvious that I had made a lasting impression on him.

The next day, I tried to change my dad's mind about selling CJ, but he wouldn't give in. He told me that the choices we make affect us for the rest of our lives, and it was true. Had I not strung out my relationship with Erik, I would not have become pregnant, or had to give up my beloved horse. Feeling defeated, I walked up to the horse pasture, and wrote a letter to CJ. Not that he would ever understand it, but it helped me come to terms with what was happening that evening. My letter to my horse read,

"Dear CJ,

I will never forget the first time I laid eyes on you. You

Majoring in Motherhood

were the most beautiful horse I'd ever seen with your smooth white mane and tail, and crystal blue eyes. I knew you were meant to be mine. We have been together for almost 3 years now, and I never dreamed I would have to let you go. Pictures hang on my wall of you and me, and they hold memories that will never be forgotten. You helped me break loose from the world every time I rode you, and you would free me from what hurt me most without ever judging me. Sure, we would butt heads all the time, and you always won that battle by bucking me off, but I was never afraid of you. I always got right back on. You taught me courage and strength every time that I had to hold on for dear life as you bucked, but you were also my friend. I told you secrets no one else knew, and you were always there for me on my worst days. You taught some of my friends how to ride, and I loved seeing the smile on their faces from the joy you gave them. You will be missed forever by me, and our memories will never be lost, but it is time to let go. I can't afford a horse and a newborn baby, and I can't take care of both of you. You deserve so much more than that. Maybe by some chance, we will meet again. I love you with all my heart. CJ, you are a great horse, and I hope you live out a great life. Farewell, my old friend."

A tear trickled down my cheek, as I sealed the letter shut. I would never open it again, and I would never again

Majoring in Motherhood

come face to face with my horse. I watched him drink from the pond, as the sunlight sparkled on his white body. He meant so much to me, and he gave me memories that I would have forever. I stood up and called out to him, watching him alert his ears in my direction. He came trotting over to me, and lowered his head in my hands.

"I love you, buddy," I said.

He snorted water all over my hands, and nibbled at my face with his slobbery lips. I laughed, and wiped the water from my hands onto my jeans.

"Well, I have to go back inside now," I said, "I have a baby that needs me." CJ looked at me one final time, and then took off running toward the back of the pasture. He had understood me.

"Farewell, my old friend," I whispered. "Farewell."

Later that day, Sam, Megan, and I all met up as we had planned, and made the depressing road trip to CJ's auction. Sam sat in the back seat with baby Noah, while I sat up front with Megan, and gave her directions. Sam played with Noah the entire trip, and he even fed him a bottle! I was shocked at how quickly he bonded with Noah, and how he treated him in such a caring way. Honestly, it was completely beyond me, because I had never seen anything like it.

When we got to the auction, Sam held Noah, and told me to go spend my last few minutes with my horse. Megan

Majoring in Motherhood

followed after me, and we stood in the round pen beside CJ, petting him, and talking sweetly to him. He was the prettiest horse at the entire auction with his glittery white coat and sparkling blue eyes. He stood out like a diamond among all the average looking horses, and his muscles flexed all over his pristine figure, making him look like a power house. I fought back my tears, as numerous people walked around CJ, making offers on him. This was going to be harder than I had ever imagined.

By the end of the night, a teenage girl had bought my beloved horse. I saw her eyes sparkle the same way mine had when she laid her eyes on him, and I knew he was all hers after that. As my father made me hand over CJ's papers to his new owners, I couldn't help but flinch with severe jealousy, since she was going to be the new owner of my ever so cherished horse. I kept telling myself that CJ was going to a better place, but it was hard to accept the circumstances. He was my best friend, and I had promised him that we would always have each other, but that was now a lie. I walked him toward the girl's horse trailer, and paused. Before I loaded him into it, I took a moment to take in one last breath of CJ. I'll never forget that familiar scent. He smelled so sweet, like clover on a misty morning. As I stared into CJ's calm blue eyes, a moment of pain went over me. This was the end of CJ and I. Our time together had been sanctified and unforgettable, but it was

Majoring in Motherhood

now time to part ways. I ran my hand down his glossy white coat, as a tear secretly crept its way down my flushed cheek. When I hugged him, he wrapped his head over my shoulder, like he knew this was goodbye. I held on tight, and for a second, the world stopped. I was caught in between a world of bitter pain, and a world of a fresh start. As I let go of CJ and his new owners took him over, I felt my heart rip in half. Our journey had so abruptly ended.

I walked back to the car in tears, and Sam wrapped his arms around me, and told me it would be alright. He reminded me that I had a beautiful baby who needed me more than anything, and told me that these hard times only last so long. I stared up into his deep brown eyes, and felt him pull at my heart strings. As God was closing the door to CJ, he was also opening the window to Sam.

Chapter Eighteen
Falling in Love

My quick relationship with Sam was surprising, yet light hearted and fun. There was never a day that we weren't happy to be with each other, and Noah became very attached to the man he came to know as his father. Within just a few short weeks, we were all completely inseparable, and a happy little family. Sam took on the responsibilities of raising Noah with me without any hesitation or grief, and he settled himself into the father role like a champ. He helped me care for Noah so well that my parents even allowed him to move in with us after just a short eight weeks of dating. It was amazing to watch how quickly Noah came to know Sam as his father, and how excited that little baby got the moment he entered the room. Noah would grin and babble, until Sam finally picked him up and played with him. At that point, I knew in my heart that I was going to marry Sam, and I knew he felt the exact same way. We were drawn to each other in a way that I can't describe, and he filled the hole that had been left in my heart.

Sam would hold me so close to him that I could feel his heart beating against my chest, and he made me feel more

Majoring in Motherhood

secure than I ever had before. He inspired me, loved me unconditionally, and always stood beside me no matter what the consequences were. I knew he was going to be the one I kissed goodnight for the rest of my lifetime. At only nineteen, I had found the love of my life.

As Noah got older, I was able to get more into the swing of things, and Sam was right there beside me the whole time. We learned what his different cries meant, and how to properly take care of him. He was such a pretty baby, and quite big for his age. I got many compliments on him everywhere we went, and people where always shocked to find out that he was much younger than they had assumed. Every mile stone that Noah reached made me a prouder mother, and as he grew older, I cherished the memories that each day held.

Noah got his first tooth at six months old on Valentine's Day, and his second tooth just one week later. The teething process was no fun, as he angrily fussed with painful gums, but he always made up for it with his blissful little personality. He loved to lie on the ground and roll around actively. You couldn't turn your back on him for five seconds, because by the time you turned back around, he would have rolled halfway across the room. The first solid food he ever tried was a pickle, and boy did he love it! He reached for it one afternoon, while I was eating lunch, so I thought, "*why not?*" I expected him to cry from the bitter

Majoring in Motherhood

sourness, but instead, he gnawed happily at the pickle, until it was gone. He was always surprising me with something new every day, and I loved him so dearly. He always screamed happily, and gave the biggest smiles to anyone who acknowledged him, and he brought happiness into the lives of people that needed it more than we knew. Each day a different person would stop me to see my baby, with his fiery red hair, blue eyes, and big smile. Every person had a different story to tell, and sometimes, Noah helped heal the grief in someone's life for a split second without even realizing it. His big happy smiles welcomed different people into our lives every day, and he was my pride and joy.

Sam and I got more into the swing of being a family too, and we developed a daily routine. I would go to my college classes in the mornings, while Sam stayed with Noah, and then when I got home, Sam would head out for his evening job. Everything was falling into place the way it was meant to, and our relationship was growing stronger and stronger with every passing day.

Mid-terms were in session at school, and students were stressing out trying to pass all their exams. Sam studied with me every night, but our studying always turned into playing with Noah. He was our entire lives, and even though I was doing my best to get through college, I realized that for the next eighteen years, I would be

Majoring in Motherhood

majoring in motherhood. Even with all the distractions of a baby, I passed all my exams with flying colors, and glanced forward into an adventurous spring break with my little family. Because we were parents, Sam and I couldn't attend the many parties that were taking place, but we didn't care. We just wanted to be together, and that's exactly what we did. We took Noah to the beach for the first time, and he experienced the feeling of the sand between his toes, and the waves crashing against the shore. When it was time for Noah's nap, Sam and I would lay on the couch, and just talk for hours.

"I never want to let you go, baby," he said one afternoon. I brushed his hair out of his eyes, and stared at him. He had such beautiful big brown eyes.

"Baby, you will never have to let me go. I will always belong to you, because I love you," I replied softly.

"Are you positive you love me? I'm so afraid you're going to get tired of me one day."

I could sense a tone of fear in Sam's voice, and I wanted nothing more than to show him how much he meant to me. He had nothing to be afraid of, because I could never get tired of him. He was the closest friend I'd ever had, and he treated me with a kindness I had never known before. He truly was in love with me, and I could feel the love he held inside. It was real.

"Baby, I love you so much that it hurts sometimes. I

Majoring in Motherhood

have never loved before, now that I know what love really feels like, and you mean so much to me," I replied.

A huge grin of relief spread across his face. No one else could take my breath away the way Sam did. He was my one and only, and I was his. I lived, breathed, and dreamed Sam. I knew without one single doubt that he was the one. Everything he did pointed in the direction to marriage. He was so important to both Noah and I, and our lives wouldn't be the same without him. He treated Noah with genuine love, and he had been in Noah's life, since he was only five weeks old. He would continually play with Noah, until he laughed himself silly, and rock him sweetly to sleep at night. He was meant to stay in our lives to be my husband and Noah's daddy. I had a feeling in my heart that one day, he would adopt Noah. God wouldn't make him such an influential part of Noah's life for no reason.

After only six months of dating, we were completely sure that we wanted to spend the rest of our lives together, and get married. We both knew deep in our hearts that we had something special, and it would last forever. Sam decided that he wanted to join the military, because we were so serious about marriage, and it would set up our entire lives for us. He told me that it was the smartest thing for us to do as a young family, and I supported his decision with all my heart. He was going to join the Coast Guard. At that point, I knew I needed to be strong for him, even

Majoring in Motherhood

though the fact that I would lose Sam for months at a time to deployments was eating my heart out. I would stand beside him no matter what, and he knew that, even though nothing scared me more than the thought of being without him.

The next week, Sam took his ASVAB test for the military, and scored exceptionally well. His score was high enough that he qualified for every job available in the Coast Guard, and he got to choose whichever one he wanted. I was so proud of the man that was going to become my husband, and promised him my support in everything he did. That night, we stood in my driveway, discussing our future lives. Sam was serious about taking this next step in becoming a family. He saw the Coast Guard as the best decision for our situation, as he could also obtain his college funds, the best medical insurance, and housing for our family from joining the service. We talked long and hard about the pros and cons we would encounter, and how we would overcome them together.

"Baby, are you sure you will be able to handle all the days that I won't be with you and Noah?" he asked. I drug my shoe across the ground, and took a moment to think. I knew I could handle them, I just didn't want to, but I would do anything for Sam.

"I'm willing to handle the lonely nights without you, the tears I will cry, the Valentine's Day I spend alone, and the

Majoring in Motherhood

pain I'll feel from missing you, because I am so lucky to have a man like you to miss," I said. I took a moment to accept how much things were going to change, before I continued. "I will never find another man who could ever take your place in my heart." Sam's face lit up with confidence, and his eyes glimmered in the pale moonlight.

"Forever," he said.

"Forever," I promised.

At that point, we made it known that we were becoming engaged, and began the search for our wedding rings. We only had a few short months, before Sam was going to be shipped out for boot camp, and we planned a wedding as quickly and effectively as we could. Ultimately, all that mattered to us was vowing ourselves to each other forever, and never breaking that promise, and that's exactly what we planned to do. After several weeks of trying on wedding rings, and picking out our favorites, Sam proposed to me with the most *beautiful* wedding ring I had ever seen. I said yes immediately, and threw myself into his arms. This was official.

A few weeks later, I was able to convince my mother to go wedding dress shopping with me. I was full of energy on the ride to the bridal boutique. Mom was questioning what kind of wedding dress I sought out, and I was able to answer without any hesitation. I had my perfect dress in mind, and nothing would alter my man hunt for the perfect

Majoring in Motherhood

wedding dress! Once we got to the bridal boutique, we had to wait around for almost an hour, until someone could get around to helping us. Being a Saturday afternoon, the place was bustling with other eager brides seeking a beautiful wedding dress. Finally, it was my turn. My mother and I walked around looking at dresses, while Noah played with toys in his stroller. He was such a simple baby, and so easily amused. He peered around at the many dresses in the store that ranged from shades of white to ivory, and at all the sparkly and wonderful things. His eyes were curious with young imagination. As I continued to look at dresses, both my mother and I landed on a particular one. It stood out among the rest in the purest shade of white, and had the most beautiful train that trailed behind its many layers of soft fabric. It was just the dress I had pictured in my mind; strapless and flowing. I was more than impatient to try it on. After a while, a dressing room opened up, and you can bet that I was the first one to grab it. It was exactly the wedding dress I had envisioned. It fit my body like a glove, showing off my slender figure, and was the perfect shade of white to accompany my fair skin tone. It was a ball gown style dress with layers of beautiful organza fabric that swept behind it when the wind blew. We matched it with a glittery chapel length veil that cascaded down my entire body, and a hairband that was decorated with sparkles and white feathers. Everyone in the boutique

Majoring in Motherhood

stopped to stare. All of the wedding consultants agreed that most women could not pull off the dress, but that I absolutely rocked it. My mother's eyes glazed over with tears, as she looked me up and down. This was *the* dress.

My mother called my father to tell him we had found the dress, but he was not as thrilled as she expected. He told her to wait to buy the dress, until Sam's military contract came through, because without one, there was no reason for us to get married just yet. We couldn't support ourselves, and he didn't want us living in his home married. I completely understood where my father was coming from, so I didn't argue with him. We already knew that Sam's contract was coming through, and that was the only dress they had left in that style, so I bought the dress without any hesitation. I knew I would never find a dress that beautiful again, and it didn't need one single alteration, because it fit me perfectly. It also turned out that the dress was on a huge sale price, so I went home extremely happy. What a blessing! It seemed as though God was helping our wedding along, and silently, I thanked him. My father agreed to reimburse me for my wedding dress expenses, after he saw Sam's signed contract, and that was fair enough.

A few months before our wedding, a tragedy hit the gulf coast known as the infamous "BP Oil Spill." My heart went out to all the innocent sea birds, fish, dolphins, and

Majoring in Motherhood

sea turtles that would suffer the devastating effects of the gushing oil rig, and Sam and I decided that we were going to do anything that we could to help out. Without any hesitation, Sam got some time off work, and we set a date on the calendar to go volunteer with the animals harmed in the oil spill.

We hooked up with a small marine rescue group who assigned Sam and I to care for nine sea turtles. It was heartbreaking to see the miserable depression that the sea turtles exhibited. They weren't oblivious animals, and they knew they had been taken away from their beloved homes under the sea. It was almost careless how the rescue group treated the sea turtles. They fed the sea turtles as much fish and shrimp as they wanted, and supplemented them with a vitamin, but nothing else other than that. The rescue group had beautiful facilities full of huge aquarium sized salt water tanks that stayed vacant. The sea turtles were housed in narrow black buckets that were supposed to have functioned as horse troughs, and they hardly ever got to stretch their fins in the whale sized tanks. The caretakers of the turtles didn't want to waste their time letting them swim longer than ten minutes, because they had more important things to do, such as try to impress the public with their well taken pictures of the jailed sea turtles. I was in complete objection to this, but I quietly kept to my job.

As I was volunteering, I overheard a few of the staff

Majoring in Motherhood

members talking, and I realized that the government was paying back the rescue group for every hour that a volunteer worked. I had already questioned this, because they didn't need volunteers at all! They had a full staff of employees who appeared to do nothing other than sit on their butts, while the volunteers did all their work for them. They were only calling out volunteers, because the government paid them money every time a volunteer came out to help, and they could get the volunteers to do all their work for them, while they just sat around! I grew furious. I couldn't believe that a reputable little rescue group like this was just soliciting volunteers to get more money.

Later that day, a dead dolphin was brought in to the clinic, and they asked me to help them with the necropsy. Reluctantly, I agreed. When I entered the laboratory, there was a gorgeous baby dolphin laid out on the table. I immediately knew this was going to be difficult for me, because I have such a huge love for dolphins. I pulled a bodysuit over my clothes, pulled my hair back, put on a face mask, and pulled on two pairs of gloves. The laboratory was unventilated and hot, and we all stood around sweating in our layers of clothes waiting for the veterinarian to show up. Finally, after an hour of sweating, she showed up along with a few other volunteers. Immediately, the other volunteers scoffed at me, and began barking commands at me like they were in charge. I was

Majoring in Motherhood

blown away by the way they treated me, but quietly held back my yearning to punch them in the face. As I watched the veterinarian make incisions in the beautiful dolphin, I grew even more upset. I couldn't believe I was just standing here, witnessing a dead dolphin get mutilated. I mean, I know it was something that needed to be done, but I didn't expect to have to take part in it. I listened to the veterinarian and the other volunteers discuss a case they were going to build against BP with the chunks of dolphin flesh. Were they just using this baby dolphin as another way to get money, or did they actually care that a young dolphin died as a result of the oil dispersants that were being dumped into the ocean? As I continued to watch the procedure, the smell of quickly rotting flesh grew almost unbearable, and as hot as the laboratory was, it was almost enough to make me pass out. I stared at the gelatinous bloody mess on the table that was once a free swimming dolphin, and tried to fight back the tears that were building in my eyes. As the volunteers unrelentingly kept pushing me around, and I continued to watch this baby dolphin get sliced into nothing more than just a pile of bloody dolphin steaks, I couldn't take anymore. I had been here over three hours in complete torture, and I was done! I took my gloves off, grabbed my shoes, and took off running out of the laboratory. Enough was enough, and I was never coming back to volunteer again!

Majoring in Motherhood

Sam was completely blown away when I told him how awful my experience had been, so he had to find out for himself. The next day, he went to volunteer, and returned home with the same accusations I had. We were appalled. We decided that we weren't going to go back to volunteer, because it wasn't in the best interest of those poor sea turtles, or the dead dolphins. It was in the financial interest of the rescue group, and we had no respect left for them. After experiencing such things, my deep desire to start a marine mammal rescue group stormed even harder in my heart, and I vowed to myself that I would do things different one day. I would change things, and I *truly* would help support the animals that existed beneath the surface of our bottomless oceans.

Chapter Nineteen
A New Life

Noah was now nearly a year old, had a mouthful of teeth, was eating toddler foods, and beginning to talk. His first word had been "Da-da," but he was not talking about Erik, it was for Sam. It was almost as though when Sam entered our lives, Erik just faded away. He never once wanted to see Noah, or use his visitation, and had completely moved on with his life. God knew that I was a protective hawk over Noah, and taking him away from me would be like tearing my heart right out of my chest. I am thankful that he never made me endure a single night without my son.

I wondered what it felt like to walk in Sam's shoes, and deal with becoming a father without notice, and fall in love with a girl like me. I bet I drove him crazy sometimes. What went on in that head of his? I would never know, but one thing I did know is that he loved Noah and I more than he could ever tell us. It was a genuine love that I could see; one that spoke louder than words, and shined through all our doubt. I began to drift off in thought about actually becoming his wife. I thought about the deployments Sam may receive, and how I would survive them. Would I just

Majoring in Motherhood

fall to pieces when he left? I knew I had to be there for Noah and any other babies we would have, but I was scared to be without him, especially now that my whole world depended on him.

A few weeks later, it was Noah's first birthday, and it suddenly dawned on me how quickly he was growing up. He had started out a warm little handful of baby that couldn't even hold his head up, then had progressed into an infant that was crawling all over the place, and now he was a one year old, learning how to talk, drinking from a Sippy cup, and taking his first steps. Where had the time gone? My sweet little bundle of joy was growing up so quickly, and there wasn't a thing I could do to slow him down.

Noah's birthday party was decorated head to toe in *Sesame Street*, since that had been what my first birthday was decorated in, and I made sure he got lots of toys and goodies. Noah had a blast opening presents, and playing with all his new toys. He fell in love with a yellow ball that was given to him by Sam's grandmother, and no other toy could match its pure awesomeness. I helped Noah open up presents that had flashing lights, bright colors, and made cool sounds, but he just pushed them away, and reached for the yellow ball again. I couldn't put my finger on what he liked about it so much, but he never let it leave his sight for the entire birthday party. When it was time for cake, we all gathered around and sang "happy birthday" to Noah, but he

Majoring in Motherhood

completely ignored us. He had his eyes glued to that one flickering candle in the middle of his cake, and tried to grab it as much as he could. He lunged for it numerous times, but finally realized that Mommy wasn't going to let him touch it. I cut Noah a huge slice of cake, and put it on a plate in front of him. He looked up at me for reassurance, and then dug his hands into the cake. After he had a taste of how delicious it was, he shoved it into his mouth as fast as he could, and then tilted his plate up in the air to make sure that he got every last crumb into his mouth. Now that's how you eat birthday cake! I made sure to take lots of pictures, because my little baby would never turn one again. He was growing up, and the clock would never rewind back to that day.

Just like Noah's first birthday, our wedding day came and went faster than we expected, but none the less, it was beautiful. My parents gave us the best wedding we could have asked for, and I wouldn't have changed a single thing. It was a small intimate wedding in a beautiful historic church in downtown Collierville, which had just been restored, and we were the very first couple to get married in it. That was very special to us, and we promised to stay married forever.

As I walked down the aisle to my future, I realized that this was a never-ending love. I had found life in a man who was never going to leave me, and his love was

Majoring in Motherhood

unconditional. I looked up at Sam, whose eyes sparkled full of devotion for me, and the rest of the world faded away. I felt all my worries, doubt, and fear wash out of my body, and my troubled heart was finally left to rest. For a split moment, I parted from this world, and had a brief moment with God. I could feel his forgiveness surrounding me, and it was evident that I was finally headed down the right path. It felt like I drifted down the aisle to Sam, and my eyes never left his. My prayers had been answered, and this was my proof that God existed. He had given me the one true thing I had ever really prayed for in my whole life, a husband.

Being married to Sam was the most wonderful thing in the world to me. He was by my side all the time, and it was like a breath of fresh air to wake up next to him every morning. Our relationship was strong, and I had faith that we could get through any obstacle that life threw at us. Unfortunately, Sam was shipped out for boot camp just one month after we got married, but I knew that it was necessary. This was the start of the rest of our lives.

The next few months of life were extremely lonely, and I felt like a fish out of water. Sam was at boot camp, and I could have no contact with him except for letters once a week, and my best friend, Megan, moved all the way to Florida to be with her boyfriend. Noah and I would wait excitedly at the mailbox every Thursday, in hopes that we

Majoring in Motherhood

had received a long letter from Sam, because life without him just wasn't the same. It was just Noah and I, and we spent every single day together. I took him everywhere with me, and we were the best of pals. A day without Noah was like a morning without a sunrise, or a bowl of cereal with no milk. That little baby of mine just made my day, and I loved his warm company. Without it, I sure would have been one lonely girl.

Finally, Sam was done with training, and it was time to go get him! Flying out to New Jersey to pick up Sam was one of the best times of my life. I remember how nervous I was as I got ready that morning, and we made our way to his boot camp graduation. He was part of the drill team, and the moment I first saw him again, I cried hysterically. It was overwhelming how much I had missed him, and how sudden it seemed that he was finally coming home again. He looked fearlessly handsome in his military uniform, standing tall and proud, as they marched around the gymnasium and performed with their rifles.

Finally, after the graduation was over, and everyone had received their orders, the audience was permitted to greet their loved ones. I jumped off the bleachers like a maniac, and went looking for Sam everywhere, as people cried and hugged their loved ones all around me. There were so many different faces, but none of them were Sam. Suddenly, someone grabbed my arm, and yanked me

Majoring in Motherhood

towards them. As I turned around, I saw Sam's handsome face, and I ran into his arms, as I fought back tears. He held me tight to his chest, and the madness around us completely faded away. I was back in his arms again where I was supposed to be.

We ended up getting stationed in Honolulu, Hawaii, and the military moved us out there just one week after Sam's graduation. He was assigned to a large Coast Guard cutter, and was deployed only four months after our arrival, leaving me thousands of miles away from any friends or family. The deployment was tremendously hard on me, since I had yet to meet any other military wives, and took care of Noah alone with no one to talk to. I even managed to completely move us out of our tiny apartment in downtown Honolulu, and into safer housing on a military base. All of this helped me to stay busy while Sam was gone, but nothing could fight the lonely days and sleepless nights I encountered. What helped ease the pain of missing Sam was that just a few weeks before his departure, we found out that we were expecting another baby. It brought me a sense of peace to know that I had a part of him there with me.

Majoring in Motherhood

Chapter Twenty
I Would Do It All Over Again

During my entire pregnancy, Sam firmly established to me that our baby would be another boy. He told me that he knew without a doubt that we would be having another boy, and nothing would change his mind. At times, I liked to think that I might be having a girl, but as Sam had so assuredly predicted, it turned out that I *was* unquestionably pregnant with another baby boy. I couldn't understand Sam's sixth sense about what the gender of our baby had been, but I didn't question it, since he hadn't failed to be right.

We decided upon the name Luke for our son, and I was content that Noah would have a brother to grow up with. The pregnancy dragged on slowly, and by the ninth month, I was more than ready to get Luke out of my stomach. I was carrying this baby much heavier than I had carried Noah, and it was causing me severe pain in my hips and lower back. My obstetrician predicted that Luke would weigh about seven and a half pounds, and urged me to walk as many miles as I could every day to help bring on labor.

Sam returned home from deployment just in time to help me prepare for the birth of Luke, and I went into labor

Majoring in Motherhood

about a month later. I woke up to Sam putting on his uniform around five o'clock in the morning with some nasty contractions, but I wasn't sure if I was in labor just yet. Without thinking much about it, I kissed Sam goodbye, and told him to have a good day at work. As Sam got into his car to leave, I had a contraction hit me so hard that I had no doubt in my mind that our baby was on its way. I jumped out of bed and wobbled down the stairs as quickly as a pregnant girl can, trying to catch Sam before he left. I rushed out the front door, and luckily, I was able to wave Sam down before he drove off. My mother had been staying with us, waiting on Luke to make his arrival, and we quickly packed our bags, and dropped Noah off with his babysitter. As the three of us were making our way to the hospital, the contractions started coming faster and faster, and soon, they were coming every two minutes. Suddenly, once we had reached the hospital, my labor completely stalled. When we got into the maternity ward, the doctors monitored me for contraction; however, there were none at all. Seeing that I was not in active labor, the doctor began discharging me from the hospital to send me home, but my mother objected.

"She's been in a lot of pain. I think you should check her cervix," she insisted. The doctor gave my mother a haughty look, and sighed provocatively as he went to check my cervix. Suddenly, he raised his eye brows, and a

Majoring in Motherhood

surprising look spread across his face.

"You are definitely not leaving this hospital," he ordered.

"Why not? What's going on?" I asked.

"Surprisingly, you are almost eight centimeters dilated," he replied. I raised my eye brows the way he had, followed by Sam and my mother. We couldn't believe that I was already that far along in labor, and I was lucky that I had reached the hospital when I did. The doctor informed me that I must be in the middle of a stalled labor, where all contractions completely stop out of the blue. He told me he was going to eat some lunch, and ordered me to go to the food court with Sam and my mother to eat as well. I thought it was strange that he was sending me three floors down to the food court to eat when I was eight centimeters dilated, but I didn't argue. By the time I had made it to the elevator, I was doubling over in pain, and the contractions had returned full force. Sam and my mother sat down at Subway to eat their sandwiches, while I gripped the table in pain, and blurted out cusswords.

"I can't believe I'm in fucking labor, and they send me to eat at Subway!" I screamed. "What hospital sends a girl in labor to fucking Subway?!"

Mom and Sam laughed at my rashness, while I doubled over in pain at the table. Normally, my mother would have scolded me for using such foul language, but I think she

Majoring in Motherhood

was just as baffled as I was that they sent us to the food court. The doctor obviously knew what he was doing though, because when I returned to the maternity ward, my labor was in full swing. I gave birth to Luke three hours later, and he ended up weighing a whopping nine pounds and three and a half ounces.

My mother stayed with me, until Luke was about two weeks old, and then she flew the ten hour flight back to Memphis. Then about a week after that, Sam was deployed again, and I was left alone with just my two sons. I grew to appreciate the company I had from my newborn and Noah, but it never failed to be difficult trying to get through each day alone. Taking care of a two year old and a newborn at the same time wasn't easy, but I did the best I could to make sure that each of their needs were met. I embraced each day with them, and my two little boys became my absolute best friends. I knew that if I was in a heap of sadness on the floor from a hard day, I could rely on a gentle hug from Noah to bring me back around again.

It has been difficult not always having Sam here to spend my everyday life with, but I always hold on to the love that we have together, and it keeps me sound. We have struggled through some difficult situations together, but have always managed to make it out alive in the end. Each deployment brings us closer together, and reminds us that we are lucky to have each other to miss. Sam is my

Majoring in Motherhood

best friend in the entire world, and there is nothing that could ever compare to the support and love that he provides me with each day. Every email and every phone call that I get from him make this whole job worth doing, because I know that life won't always be this hard. We won't always be miles and miles away from each other, and we won't always spend Christmas and New Year's alone. The life that we have chosen is extremely challenging for a young couple like us, but even still, I wouldn't trade it for anything in the world. God has his eye on our family, and watches out for us every single day. He mended the broken life I once had, and replaced it with genuine peace. Without God, I don't know where I would be, and I wouldn't want to know.

Noah is now almost three years old, and is my favorite little pal. He brings me so much joy, and has his own little playful personality. I love him with all my heart, and I pray every day that I can put the world at his feet, and provide him with every opportunity that I can. Luke is almost a year old, and has grown into a huge and loveable little baby. He has the same big smiled face that Noah had, and is already the size of a linebacker. Watch out NFL, because here he comes!

I will never stop working at being the best mother I can be to Noah and Luke, and I pray that I can raise them into two fine young men. No matter how hard things have

Majoring in Motherhood

been, I would go through this storm all over again for them, and I wouldn't change a thing. I have completed two years of college, and plan to finish my final two years once we are re-stationed again. As for Erik, he has never been around, and got kicked out of the Navy after only one year of service. After not paying child support for over an entire year, he eagerly had all of his parental rights terminated, and Sam has just adopted Noah as his own son. Noah has always been Sam's, and Sam has always been nothing else but Noah's father. He has raised him since he was a month old, and will continue to love and raise him for the rest of his life, along with Luke. I believe that God brought each of us together to be a family, and I am happy that I finally listened to God's quiet hints that I wasn't headed down the right path in my life. I pray that my children will never go through what I've been through, but more importantly, I hope they always know that I will love them no matter what.

I have come to terms with the answer that there is a season for everything. There was a rich season in which I made fond memories of my horse, CJ. There was a season for having friends, and growing into the person I am today. There was a season for my pregnancy, and there was a season for the moment I realized I had to truly become a woman. There was a season for finding the man I am supposed to be with forever. There will be a season for

Majoring in Motherhood

motherhood and raising our children, and there will be a season for letting them go. This is my true story, and it is written to express my deepest feelings to the ones I care so intensely for. Nothing matters more to me than for the ones I love so dearly to know how much I care about them, and how much they have influenced my life. This is not the end of my story, it's just the beginning...

Acknowledgments

Most importantly, I would like to thank God for taking control of my crummy life, and rescuing me from the hell I was living in. He changed my world, and helped push me to finish this book, so that I could get His message out there. God is real. He is true. And he's just a prayer away.

I would like to thank my sweetheart, Sam, for being there for me through this entire process, and always supporting me no matter what. I promised you my heart when I said "I do," and that promise I will keep forever. I was writing this book long before I met him, he just changed the ending...

I would like to give an especially important thank you to my son, Noah Michael. If it wasn't for him, I wouldn't have been so dedicated to writing this book, and to let him know how loved he is. He deserves to have the world at his feet, and that's just what I plan to give him.

Majoring in Motherhood

To my wonderful parents, Tim and Nancy, I know I have made many mistakes through these last difficult years, but you were always there to help guide me back on the right path. Thank you for being such amazing parents, and always being there to influence me to do better in my own life. I know you weren't ready for a grandbaby just yet, but you have helped bear the burden of a baby greater than anyone I know. I love you both so much, and nothing will ever change that.

I would also like to thank my grandparents, Barbara and John Foreman. Grandma and Papaw, you have always been there for me when I needed a little nudge of encouragement. You have never sent me in the wrong direction, and you have always shown me such unconditional love. I love you so much, and I appreciate everything you have done for me, big and small.

About the Author

Barbra Williams is a young military wife, currently living in Hawaii with her husband, Sam, their two sons, Noah and Luke, and their dog, Jake. She spends her time writing, being a mother and wife, and vows to return to her passion of horseback riding when life will allow her to. This is her first novel.

Majoring in Motherhood

*Love is patient, love is kind. It does not envy, it does not boast, it is not proud. It is not rude, it is not self-seeking, it is not easily angered, it keeps no record of wrongs. Love does not delight in evil, but rejoices with the truth. It always protects, always hopes, always perseveres.
Love never fails.
I Corinthians 13:4-8*

Majoring in Motherhood

My horse, CJ

Majoring in Motherhood

The Pregnancy

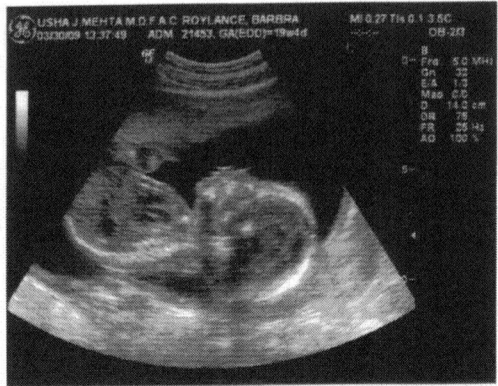

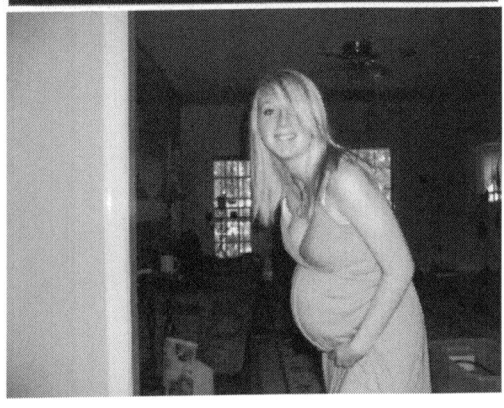

Majoring in Motherhood

Noah as a baby

Majoring in Motherhood

Noah today

Majoring in Motherhood

Our Family

Majoring in Motherhood

My Husband Sam

Majoring in Motherhood

Coming Home from Deployment

Majoring in Motherhood

Baby Luke

Majoring in Motherhood

*For you created my inmost being; you knit me together in my mother's womb. I praise you because I am fearfully and wonderfully made; your works are wonderful,
I know that full well. My frame was not hidden from you
when I was made in the secret place.
When I was woven together in the depths of the earth, your eyes saw my unformed body.
All the days ordained for me
were written in your book
before one of them came to be.*

Psalm 139:13-16

Majoring in Motherhood

Trust in the Lord with all your heart, and lean not on your own understanding; In all your ways acknowledge him, and he shall direct your paths.

Proverbs 3:5-6

A note from the author:

I wrote this book to show other young women just how hard being a young parent truly is, and how deeply it affects your life. If just one teen takes the time to read this book, and takes the precaution to avoid situations like this, then I've done my job. I also wrote this book to show my son that no matter how messy things were, it was not his fault, and I will always love him unconditionally. I will do everything I can to put the world at his feet, and he's been the best thing that ever happened to me. I would go through this storm all over again just for him.

Barbra Williams can be contacted at:

MajoringInMotherhood@yahoo.com

Be watching for her next release!

Made in the USA
Lexington, KY
26 August 2012